How To Explore Your College Options:
A Workbook for High School Students

Regina H. Paul and Marie G. Segares
Co-Hosts of *USACollegeChat*

A publication of

Policy Studies in Education
A nonprofit organization with over 40 years of success
in engaging parents and school boards in K–12 education

How To Explore Your College Options: A Workbook for High School Students by Regina H. Paul and Marie G. Segares

Copyright © 2017 by Regina H. Paul and Marie G. Segares. *All rights reserved.*

Cover photographs by David Mark, Yaqub Shabazz, and Foundry Co.

Permission is granted by the publisher to reproduce worksheets in the appendices for individual use only. No other part of this book may be reproduced, stored in a retrieval system, or transmitted in any form or by any means—written, electronic, mechanical, recorded, photocopied, or otherwise—without the prior written permission of one of the authors, Regina H. Paul or Marie G. Segares, or of the publisher, Policy Studies in Education.

Books may be purchased in quantity by contacting the publisher, Policy Studies in Education, by mail (P. O. Box 220212, Great Neck, New York 11022) or by email (info@policystudies.org).

Published by: Policy Studies in Education, Great Neck, New York

Library of Congress Control Number: 2017938944
ISBN 978-0-9864088-2-3 (ebook)
ISBN 978-0-9864088-3-0 (print book)
10 9 8 7 6 5 4 3 2 1
1. Education/Counseling/General
2. Family & Relationships/Life Stages/Teenagers

First Edition
Printed in the United States of America

DEDICATION

For high school students everywhere, of course

CONTENTS

Why Are We Talking to You Now?	1
Step 1: Expand Your College List	3
Step 2: Preview the College Profile Worksheet	7
Step 3: Preview College Websites and Other Sources	9
Step 4: Research the College's History and Mission	13
Step 5: Research the College's Location	19
Step 6: Research the College's Enrollment	21
Step 7: Research the College's Class Size	27
Step 8: Research the College's Academics	31
Step 9: Research the College's Schedule	37
Step 10: Research the College's Housing	39
Step 11: Research the College's Security Measures	43
Step 12: Research the College's Activities and Sports	45
Step 13: Research the College's Admission Practices	49
Step 14: Research the College's Cost	53
Now, It's Up to You	55
About the Authors	57
Appendix 1: **Your Long List of College Options**	59
Appendix 2: **College Profile Worksheet**	61

WHY ARE WE TALKING TO YOU NOW?

> **If you are a high school freshman or sophomore,** you are in the perfect spot to get a head start in the college admission game. You can use this workbook over the next couple of years to put together the best personalized research guide about colleges—ever.
>
> **If you are a high school junior,** this workbook is ideally suited for your immediate use. You should be able to use it productively at any time during your junior year and up until your college applications are finally submitted.
>
> **If you are a high school senior,** you should find this workbook helpful, too, if you still have some time before your college applications are due. But you have to hurry up! (And remember that all colleges do NOT have a January 1 deadline.)

Since 2014, we have been talking to your parents in our weekly podcast, *USACollegeChat*. The truth is that we have given them more information about colleges than anyone could probably use.

We took them on a virtual tour of colleges nationwide and profiled many public and private colleges in every region of the country to try to get them—and, of course, you—to look outside your family's geographic comfort zone when considering where you should apply.

When we put together that virtual college tour, we realized something very important: There are a lot of colleges out there, and it is impossible to keep up with what is going on at most of them.

We also realized what your biggest problem is (well, yours and theirs, actually): **You don't know anything about most colleges.** We have been doing this for a couple of decades, and there was a lot of stuff we didn't know either, as it turned out. So, how do you solve that problem?

The simple answer is just to ask a guidance counselor at your high school. You would think that guidance counselors would know quite a bit about lots of colleges and that they could pass that information on to you. Here's why that usually doesn't work.

Let's start with public high schools. As you probably already know, most public high schools don't have guidance counselors who are dedicated to working only on college counseling. That means that your guidance counselors, with caseloads in the hundreds, have to help students with college applications while dealing simultaneously with students who might be in serious personal or academic trouble. That's an overwhelming job, and that is exactly why **most high school guidance counselors cannot help you enough** when it comes to exploring many college options, narrowing them down, and finally choosing the perfect colleges to put on your list.

Some public high schools—and even more private schools—have designated one of the school's guidance counselors as a college counselor, specializing in college placement and perhaps financial aid and devoting all of his or her time to helping students undertake and complete their college searches. If your school has a college counselor like that, you are lucky indeed. Of course, searching through hundreds of colleges to find the right ones for you and then working through those college applications (including all of the essays) is the work of a lot of hours—at least 20 hours and really closer to 40 hours, we would say. Does your counselor have that much time to spend with you? Unfortunately, probably not, even if you attend a private school.

> **What if you are homeschooled?** Without the help of a school guidance counselor or college counselor—even for a very limited amount of time—you might feel more at a loss than your friends who attend public or private schools. Should you expect your parents to know everything you need to know about a wide array of college choices? No, you shouldn't. Respecting your parents' opinions about colleges is certainly important, even crucial. But it is not likely that they are experts on the many, many colleges here in the U.S. (and abroad).

All high school students need to get help from somewhere or someone. We believe that this workbook is a good way to get some. That's why we are talking to you now. We want you to have a way to find out the information you need about many colleges so that you will be in the best possible position to compare those colleges and then to make the right decision about where to apply and, eventually, about where to attend. While you will undoubtedly want and need some adult advice in thinking through the many options, **what you need first is information—and a lot of it.**

If you already have a list of colleges you are interested in, you will need information about each one of those. But, just as important, you will need information about colleges that are not yet on your list—including colleges that you have never considered because you didn't know they existed. That's not your fault now, but it will be if you don't take steps to correct it. So, let's get started.

STEP 1:
EXPAND YOUR COLLEGE LIST

This chapter focuses on something that you are just about to do totally wrong. Really, totally wrong. In fact, our advice in this chapter is probably the opposite of what many school counselors and college consultants are telling you as you start a serious consideration of where to apply, especially if you are already a senior. We bet they are telling you to start by narrowing your list of colleges, but we would like you to **start by expanding your list of colleges.**

There is plenty of time later to narrow down your options—once you get to the October or November before applications are due. While expanding your list might seem unnecessary, time consuming, or even wasteful, we believe that expanding your options now could mean the difference between an okay college choice and a great college choice for you later.

The Dreaded Geographic Comfort Zone

> There is nothing we dislike more than your "geographic comfort zone." It could be what stands between you and your best possible college choice.

So, what is it?

The great majority of high school graduates who go to college choose a college in their home state—perhaps as many as 70 percent of them. Undoubtedly, you have one or more colleges in your home state on your list of college options right now. That's okay with us. However, **what's NOT okay is to have nothing BUT colleges in your home state on your list.**

Here's why: **It's a big world out there.** There are so many intriguing colleges in it that we hate for you to limit yourself to those nearby. We hate for you to limit yourself to those that are likely to have a majority of students a lot like you from the same part of the country as you. Your first step in making a list of college options should NOT be to narrow down the choices and to close off opportunities. **You should NOT be settling either for colleges that are nearby or for colleges that you and your parents and your school counselor already know a lot about.**

We know that there are some good reasons for kids to stay close to home for college. We understand that some families want to keep their kids close to home for cultural reasons, perhaps in order to participate in family events or religious activities. We understand that some families need to have their kids stay at home in order to help with family responsibilities. Those reasons are hard to argue against.

We know that staying close to home might make going to college more affordable for some families, especially if living at home saves on housing expenses. But we also know that it is hard to know in advance how generous a financial aid package might be from an out-of-state college. Did you know that some states offer an attractive discount at their public colleges to students who come from nearby states? We bet you didn't. Check out, for example, the Midwest Student Exchange Program or the Western Undergraduate Exchange or the New England Regional Student Program, if you live in those regions of the country.

We also know that you can sometimes get into a better college when it is far from home. Why? Because almost every college likes the idea of geographic diversity in its student body. Colleges like to claim that they draw students "from all 50 states and from 100 foreign countries." You will see this kind of statement on many college websites. Pay attention, because **you might be far more attractive to a college halfway across the country than to one in your own back yard.** That's because you will give that faraway college bragging rights. This is especially true for private colleges that do not have the same mission to serve students in their own state as public colleges do.

We also know that some parents just can't imagine sending their kids away from home for the first time. In fact, you might not be able to imagine leaving home for the first time. But, we encourage you and your parents to think hard about that. Isn't college the perfect time to make that break—a time when you can live somewhere else under the supervision of college staff in relatively secure surroundings, a time when you can learn to function as an adult in a safe environment (that is, learn to manage your money, do your work, plan your time, and make new friends)?

We urge you (and your parents) to get outside your family's geographic comfort zone. You have nothing to lose at this stage in the process. Researching colleges outside your hometown, outside your state, and outside your region doesn't mean you have to attend one of them—or even apply to one of them. But it does mean that you will have the information that you need to make a better decision when the time comes.

Of course, there is always the exception that proves the rule. Here is a true story: For Polly Haas, the perfect college was actually right at home in New York City. Polly was planning to major in dance, and one of the very best colleges for dance is in her hometown—the joint **Fordham University** and Alvin Ailey American Dance Theater's B.F.A. program at Fordham's Lincoln Center Campus in Manhattan. Just to be safe, Polly applied to out-of-town colleges, too, in case she decided that she really wanted to study away from home. But, toward the end of the process, she realized that it was silly for her to be trying to LEAVE New York City when young dancers nationwide were trying to COME TO New York City. So, when she got her acceptance letter from Fordham, that was that. (P.S. Polly got her master's degree in London, so she eventually left New York City—when the time was right.)

Step 1 in researching colleges is all about how to **get outside your geographic comfort zone.** Just give it a try.

Take Step 1—Now!

Conveniently, the Bureau of Economic Analysis has divided the U.S. into eight regions:

- **Far West**—California, Nevada, Oregon, Washington, Hawai'i, Alaska
- **Rocky Mountains**—Colorado, Wyoming, Idaho, Montana, Utah
- **Southwest**—Arizona, New Mexico, Oklahoma, Texas
- **Plains**—Kansas, Missouri, Nebraska, Iowa, Minnesota, North Dakota, South Dakota
- **Southeast**—Louisiana, Arkansas, Mississippi, Alabama, Georgia, Florida, South Carolina, North Carolina, Tennessee, Kentucky, Virginia, West Virginia
- **Great Lakes**—Wisconsin, Michigan, Illinois, Indiana, Ohio
- **Mideast**—Pennsylvania, New York, New Jersey, Delaware, Maryland, District of Columbia
- **New England**—Massachusetts, Connecticut, Rhode Island, Vermont, New Hampshire, Maine

However, we thought that the Bureau stuffed too many states into the Southeast; so, **we divided the Southeast into two regions (southern and northern), and you should, too.** That will give you nine regions to investigate.

We used these nine regions when we did our virtual college tour on our podcast. **You should listen to the tour in Episodes 27 through 53 of our podcast or simply read the show notes at usacollegechat.org.** It's all **free**, so take advantage of it.

We thought hard about how you should create what we will call your **Long List of College Options**—your LLCO, for short. We decided to start with this advice:

> ✓ **Make sure that you have at least two four-year colleges in each of the nine geographic regions of the U.S. on your LLCO.**

So, that would give you at least 18 four-year colleges. But, our guess is that your list already had some regions covered with more than two colleges—especially the region you live in. That's fine. Have as many colleges on your LLCO as you like from each region. **But don't ignore any region!** That's what it means to get outside your geographic comfort zone.

How should you choose the colleges for your LLCO? Well, you probably know about some colleges already—from family, friends, school counselors, and teachers. You should discover some more from our virtual college tour, in which we talk about several hundred four-year colleges. You might find some more through a variety of online searches and quick looks at those college websites. Remember, you don't need too much information about each one just to put it on your LLCO.

You will soon see that you can learn a lot from reading a college website. Furthermore, you can learn not only about that one college, but also about colleges in general and about what to look for on the next website you go to. It's an education in itself. **You really need an education ABOUT higher education.**

By the way, don't start looking at two-year colleges, or community colleges, yet. Two-year colleges can easily be added to your LLCO closer to application time, partly because their applications are typically less demanding to complete. We are also assuming that you are most likely to attend a two-year college in or near your hometown and, therefore, you will not need to do much investigating before applying.

We do have some reservations about two-year colleges, especially for students who have just graduated from high school and are moving directly into college full time. We know that two-year colleges are a great choice for saving money and for helping kids who need a bit more maturity or a bit more academic preparation before heading into college. (And we know that two-year colleges are a great choice for adults, especially working adults, who are returning to college or starting college for the first time after being out of school for a while.) However, we worry because student graduation rates and student transfer rates from two-year colleges to four-year colleges are scandalously low, and we worry about what opportunities end up being closed off for too many kids.

But back to your LLCO. Those of you who have listened to our podcast or read the show notes know that this suggestion is coming:

> ✓ **Make sure that you have at least one college that is not in the U.S. on your LLCO.**

This is a favorite topic of ours, and we can't say enough about it. There are truly great options outside the U.S. We hope that every one of you will take advantage of studying abroad for at least a semester, no matter where you end up in college. **Studying abroad is for everyone these days**—not just for rich kids, not just for kids studying foreign languages, not just for kids at private liberal arts colleges. But you can actually study outside the U.S. for more than a semester or even for more than one year; you can simply go to a college outside the U.S. full time for four years.

You might want to check out one of our favorite options: **Richmond, The American International University in London**. Jointly accredited in the U.S. and the U.K., it is a one-of-a-kind institution. It offers students four-year bachelor's degrees—first, on an idyllic campus in Richmond-upon-Thames (just outside London) for freshmen and sophomores and, then, on an ideal Kensington campus in the heart of London for juniors and seniors. We have seen Richmond up close for a decade and still love it. (P.S. Richmond offers master's degrees, too, if you'd rather wait for your study abroad experience.) The global future is here, kids. Join it.

So, you must be up to at least 19 colleges on your LLCO—likely more. But we can't resist one last piece of advice:

> ✓ **Make sure that you have at least two public flagship universities on your LLCO—probably one from your home state plus one more.**

We say this to ensure that you have some great public options to consider. Maybe you already had them when your chose two colleges from every region, but add them if you didn't. To be clear, **we mean public "flagships," not just any public universities**—though you are also free to put other public universities on your LLCO. If you are an excellent student, the public flagship in your home state is likely to be your very best choice for a "safety school" (with some exceptions, like California, which can't accommodate all of the excellent students in their own state). **If you can't identify the public flagship in your own state or in most other states, you aren't ready to be choosing colleges yet.** Go learn about all 50 of them on our virtual college tour.

As we have said numerous times in our podcast episodes, **public flagship universities might be the hidden jewels in the college landscape.** They are often the very best place high school kids in those states can imagine going. Why? Because they are relatively inexpensive for state residents (because they are public), academically respectable (even outstanding), well regarded across the state and across the country, competitive in sports arenas, chocked full of student clubs and activities, within driving distance of home, and a social hub for lots of their high school classmates. They are often truly the place to be, if you live in that state.

As with everything, some states have better public flagship universities than others, and some public flagship universities are better funded by their states than others. Nonetheless, we are convinced that you can find at least two that you think might be great for you.

Okay, let's look at the math. We figure that you might have about 20 to 30 colleges on your LLCO. If you have more than 30, you are setting yourself up for a lot of work in completing the assignments in this workbook, but that's your decision. Now, do this:

> ✓ **Go to the Appendices at the end of this workbook and get your conveniently numbered blank LLCO (cut it out along the line on the left side of the page, if you have a print version of the workbook). Then, fill it in!**

Don't forget to ask your parents and other important family members for input about colleges that should go on your LLCO. Explain to them that this is your time to learn about many colleges so that you are better positioned to choose the right ones to apply to and, eventually, the right one to attend. Just ask them to be willing to step outside their geographic comfort zone for now.

STEP 2:
PREVIEW THE COLLEGE PROFILE WORKSHEET

Before you begin your research into the colleges on your LLCO, let's take a few minutes to preview the **College Profile Worksheet** at the back of this workbook. It outlines the critical information you should find out about each college on your LLCO before making a decision about whether to apply to that college. It's actually 11 pages long—but those pages include lots of space for you to write in!

The worksheet is going to look long to you. But this is an important decision you are about to make. In fact, we would argue that **deciding where to APPLY is just as important as deciding where to ENROLL—maybe more important.** After all, if you don't apply to a college, you can't possibly enroll there. This is the decision that sets all of the others in motion.

The **College Profile Worksheet** calls for you to make a lot of notes about colleges you are interested in. Why write all of this information down, you might be asking? Because you can't remember it. Believe us, after you research about four colleges, you will not be able to remember which college had the great bike paths and which college had the required math courses. You need a convenient way to recall each college—without having to go back to the website and look up the information again.

We learned this the hard way. When we were profiling colleges for our virtual college tour, we went back and forth to the same college website far too many times before realizing that we should have just jotted everything down the first time. We actually made a crude version of the worksheet for ourselves, and we have now improved it and put it into this workbook for you. **The College Profile Worksheet will save you lots of time in the long run.**

Here are the categories of information you will be researching about each college on your LLCO:
- ✓ **History and Mission**
- ✓ **Location**
- ✓ **Enrollment**
- ✓ **Class Size**
- ✓ **Academics**
- ✓ **Schedule**
- ✓ **Housing**
- ✓ **Security Measures**
- ✓ **Activities and Sports**
- ✓ **Admission Practices**
- ✓ **Cost**

You will see that the **College Profile Worksheet** asks you several questions in each category. Answering those questions will give you a good understanding of many important features of each college on your LLCO. As a result, you should be able to decide more efficiently and more accurately whether each college is a good match for you. So, go ahead and take Step 2:

> ✓ **Go to the Appendices at the end of this workbook and read through the College Profile Worksheet.**

Consider the questions in the worksheet as you take Step 3 in the next chapter. Eventually, you will cut out the worksheet and duplicate it so that you can fill it in for every college on your LLCO.

STEP 3:
PREVIEW COLLEGE WEBSITES AND OTHER SOURCES

Now that you know what information the **College Profile Worksheet** calls for about each of the colleges on your LLCO, we should talk about where you are going to get that information. Here are the two sources that we think are the best combination of providing lots of information and being easy to use:

1. Each college's own website
2. College Navigator, sponsored by the National Center for Education Statistics

If you are interested in looking at additional sources, you might want to check out **College Scorecard** online (https://collegescorecard.ed.gov/), sponsored by the U.S. Department of Education. Although it provides some of the information needed for the worksheet, it is more focused on college costs and what students get back in value (meaning, specifically, your earning power after graduation). College Scorecard's data might be especially helpful if your parents are, understandably, concerned about whether college is a good financial investment in your future. (P.S. **College is a good financial investment in your future—always.**)

College Websites

There is really no substitute for studying the website of each college on your LLCO. There is probably not a better way—and certainly not a cheaper way—to get more information than you could ever need about a college. Even visiting a college will not give you the range of detailed information that studying its website will.

With that said, let us point out that college websites are not created equal. Some are easy to use; some are difficult to figure out. All college websites are not set up the same way, and they do not use the same vocabulary. That is really too bad for the millions of high school students trying to use them. However, **the more you study college websites, the better you will get at finding the information you need**. The best thing to do is just get started.

Virtually every college website has a section called something like *About (the name of the college)*. You might want to start there. That section usually contains something like *Fast Facts* or *At a Glance* or *Facts and Figures*. This section gives you a quick overview of the college, and we always find it helpful and informative. This page will absolutely help you fill in the **College Profile Worksheet** for each college on your LLCO.

Most college websites include these useful sections, among others:

- *Admission*—You will spend a lot of time studying this section, obviously.
- *Academics*—If the point of college is an education, then this section is critically important, with its explanations of divisions (like undergraduate and graduate or, if it is a university, like colleges and schools), departments, majors, and minors, plus a course catalog.
- *Campus Life*, or *Student Life*—This section includes all of the things that will make up much of the rest of your life at college, including housing, dining, extracurricular activities and clubs, fraternities and sororities,

- *Athletics*—If you are looking for information on intercollegiate athletics, don't be surprised if you are automatically taken to an entirely separate website dedicated to sports (thanks to the big business that athletics is on many campuses and the boosters/fans who support the teams financially).
- *Research*—Colleges are justifiably proud of their research projects and opportunities, partly because a research university has prestige among higher education institutions. However, we find that this section is likely to be of less interest to many high school students applying for undergraduate study.

Some information you will need can be found in something called the "common data set," which you can usually find by searching a college website for it (literally, type "common data set" into the college website's search box). On many college websites, you will actually find the common data set for the most recent year as well as for previous years. On a few college websites, on the other hand, we have yet to find the common data set! (For information about the origins of the common data set, see its own website, www.commondataset.org.)

One more thing to mention about many college websites: **Take the virtual campus tour.** While these tours can take a lot longer than you might want to spend (we will forgive you if you don't look at every building that is offered), they are generally quite helpful in getting a feel for what the campus looks like—how big it is, how many buildings there are, how old the buildings are, how well landscaped the campus is, and even how spectacular or ordinary the surrounding area is. For example, just take a look at those gorgeous Rocky Mountain peaks in the background while you are on the virtual tour at the **University of Colorado Boulder**.

In our opinion, a good virtual tour gives you a lot of what a real-life campus tour does, and it is a lot cheaper and easier to take before deciding whether to apply to that college. We have noticed that high school students often notice the wrong things on live tours anyway, like whether they liked the tour guide and how comfortable they felt with the other students on the tour (who are not, please remember, students at the college). It makes sense to save your time and money for college visits until *after* you have been accepted and you have narrowed down your choices to two or three colleges, especially if you had the opportunity when you were younger to see a variety of college campuses informally.

By the way, after looking at hundreds of websites, we like **The University of Rhode Island** (URI) website quite well. So, feel free to go to www.uri.edu and take a look. You will see, for example, that the *URI At a Glance* page is crammed full of useful facts on practically every aspect of URI, and it is better presented than many we have seen.

So, here is your first assignment in Step 3:

> ✓ **Look through at least five college websites. Make sure that they are a mix of public and private institutions, of large universities and small colleges. Get familiar with the various sections that are included and the vocabulary that is used. Find the common data set. Take the virtual campus tour. Figure out how to get more efficient and effective at finding the information you want.**

College Navigator

The National Center for Education Statistics collects data from almost 7,000 colleges in the U.S. and makes those data available to you free of charge through its online tool, College Navigator (http://nces.ed.gov/collegenavigator/).

College Navigator is super easy to use. Just go to its website, type in the name of the college you are researching, and click "Show Results." **College Navigator will give you a wealth of information quickly**—more than you can actually use now or, really, ever. The thumbnail description at the top of the entry for each college includes the following:

- Address, telephone number, and college website address
- Type of institution and awards (degrees) offered
- Campus setting

- Campus housing availability
- Student population (enrollment)
- Student-to-faculty ratio

Then, there are 13 categories of information listed. The ones we think you will find most useful are these (we will talk more about each of these later):

- *Tuition, Fees, and Estimated Student Expenses*
- *Enrollment*
- *Admissions*
- *Retention and Graduation Rates*
- *Campus Security*

The other categories of information are also helpful. However, you will get more useful information about some of them by going to the college website itself, such as for *Programs/Majors*.

So, here is your second assignment in Step 3:

> ✓ **Go to College Navigator and enter the name of one of the colleges you are interested in. Browse through all of the information provided so that you get an idea of what College Navigator provides.**

You will be using information from College Navigator later, for sure. But, if you need a few more colleges for your LLCO, **you can use College Navigator right now to do a search for additional colleges** to put on your list by using any one or more of these filters:

- *State*
- *ZIP Code* (with its surrounding area, determined in miles, by you)
- *Programs/Majors*
- *Level of Award* (bachelor's or associate's)
- *Institution Type* (public, private non-profit, private for-profit; 4-year, 2-year, or <2-year)
- *Tuition & Fees*
- *Undergraduate Student Enrollment*
- *Housing*
- *Campus Setting* (rural, town, suburban, or city)
- *% of Applicants Admitted*
- *Test Scores—25th percentile*
- *Varsity Athletic Teams*
- *Extended Learning Opportunities* (distance learning, weekend/evening, credit for life experience)
- *Religious Affiliation*
- *Specialized Mission* (single-sex, historically black college or university, tribal college)

Then, just click "Show Results." From the list of colleges that comes up, you can simply choose the one or ones that you would like to consider adding to your LLCO.

What If You Do Not Have a Computer?

If you do not have a computer at home, our best advice would be to try to get access to one, perhaps at school or at a public library. We know that is easy for us to say and perhaps hard for you to do, but it will make your life easier in the long run. (Eventually, you are probably going to want to fill out the Common Application online, so figuring out computer access now might make life smoother for you later.)

In the old days, before you were born, prospective college students had attractive college catalogs (sometimes called "viewbooks") mailed to their homes. Some colleges will still do this, so don't be afraid to call and ask the Admissions Office.

When you don't have easy access to a computer at home, the completion of a College Profile Worksheet for each college on your LLCO becomes even more important. When you fill those out, you are essentially creating your own information file, which you can refer back to as often as necessary. The completed worksheets can take the place of a computer for you until it is time to submit applications.

STEP 4: RESEARCH THE COLLEGE'S HISTORY AND MISSION

Step 4 begins your research into the colleges you plan to apply to—including, of course, the one you will actually attend someday. But, first, you need to get ready to record useful information about those colleges.

> ✓ Go to the Appendices at the end of this workbook and get the **College Profile Worksheet** (cut it out along the line on the left side of the page, if you have a print version of the workbook). Now, you can duplicate it easily. Make a copy for each college on your LLCO.

With that done, you can get started.

> ✓ Pick one college from your LLCO and put that college's name at the top of page 1 of the **College Profile Worksheet**. You are all set. (It doesn't matter which college you begin with because you will research them all eventually.)

So, let's go to the first category on the worksheet: **History and Mission**. We believe that lots of students are proud of the beginnings and traditions of the college they choose to attend. In fact, **some students choose a college because of its history and its traditions**. By the way, don't forget that the reasons why a college is public or private are part of a college's history and mission. This category might mean more to you than you expect.

As you complete Step 4 by researching each college on your LLCO on its website, you will see that some colleges started out as private colleges and became public for lots of interesting reasons. Some colleges started out as single-sex colleges, serving only men or only women, and became coeducational colleges for lots of interesting reasons. Some colleges started out as faith-based colleges and became less so for lots of interesting reasons. And some colleges just have truly remarkable stories—including, for example, the many HBCUs (historically black colleges and universities) that have taken a longtime stand on behalf of the rights of African-American students to a college education. There is lots for you to learn in this category.

Brief History of the College

Here are a few stories taken from some of our favorite college histories, as told on their websites:

- **Tuskegee University**, a well-known HBCU, was founded in Alabama in 1881 by Booker T. Washington, who was the institution's first teacher and its head until his death in 1915. Washington brought George Washington Carver to Tuskegee to head its agricultural studies, and it was at Tuskegee that Carver did his work on peanuts, on sweet potatoes, on mobile classrooms to educate farmers, and more. Both Washington and Carver are buried on Tuskegee's grounds.

- When the **University of Iowa** started holding classes in 1855, 41 of its 124 students were women—one-third of the student body. UI was the first public university to award a law degree to an African American (in 1870) and to a woman (in 1873). And it was the first public university to allow an African-American athlete to play on a varsity team (in 1895). UI was also the first university to create a department of education, which became the birthplace of a number of famous standardized tests, including the ACT.
- Founded in 1791, the public **University of Vermont** is the fifth-oldest college in New England (after four Ivy League schools), and it, too, began as a private university. The Marquis de Lafayette, the French officer who fought with the rebel colonists during the American Revolution, laid the cornerstone of a building that still stands on the UVM campus. UVM also claims to be the first college with a charter that said it was nondenominational, and it was the first college to admit women and African Americans into its chapter of the Phi Beta Kappa honor society.
- The public **University of Delaware** was founded in 1743 (in Pennsylvania!) as a private academy to educate ministers and was moved to Delaware in 1765. Its first class boasted three students who went on to sign the Declaration of Independence, one of whom also signed the U.S. Constitution. UD's colors of blue and gold were taken from the Delaware State flag, which got them from the colors of George Washington's uniform. They also represent the colors of the flag of Delaware's first Swedish colonists.
- The **University of Wyoming** was founded by its territorial legislature in 1886—four years before Wyoming even became a state. The University had both female students and female faculty members from the very beginning.
- The **City University of New York** (CUNY), now with 24 campuses, began in 1849 as the Free Academy with about 200 students. CUNY has a history full of political battles over free tuition and over outreach to New York City's immigrant populations as they arrived decade after decade. Its website notes that in "the post-World War I era when discrimination against Jews was common at Ivy League universities and other private educational institutions, many Jewish students and academics found their intellectual home at New York's public colleges, where ethnicity, religion and national background barred no one."
- The second-oldest college in the U.S., the **College of William & Mary** was chartered by King William III and Queen Mary II in 1693 in the Virginia Colony. The college cut its ties with England in 1775 and became state supported in 1903. It is the home of the first Greek-letter society (Phi Beta Kappa, founded in 1776), the first student honor code, and the first law school in America.
- In 1749, Benjamin Franklin formed the Academy and Charitable School that became the **University of Pennsylvania**. Franklin served as its president and then as a trustee until 1790. His goal, considered radical for the times, was to offer something like a modern liberal arts curriculum to train students for business, government, and public service rather than for the ministry. The first medical school in the colonies was established at Penn in 1765.
- The now-renowned Jubilee Singers of **Fisk University** left their almost-bankrupt campus in 1871 to try to raise enough money to keep their HBCU open by embarking on a tour that introduced the world to traditional spirituals. They succeeded. Decades later, Charles Spurgeon Johnson, the intellectual architect of the Harlem Renaissance, became a professor at Fisk and later its first African-American president in 1946. He eventually brought to Fisk a number of Harlem Renaissance stars, like Aaron Douglas, James Weldon Johnson, and Arna Bontemps.

As you read about the history for each of the colleges on your LLCO, think about the histories you have just read. While not all college histories are this noteworthy, some might attract your attention enough to make you want to be part of their traditions.

> ✓ Go to **Question 1**. Jot down a brief history of the college.

While you are at the college website, you can easily answer **Questions 2, 3, and 4** in the **History and Mission** section.

Claims About the College

You might have noticed some "firsts" in the website's explanation of the college's history (e.g., the first public university in the South, the first college to award a bachelor's degree to a woman, etc.), but **there might be another**

section of the website devoted to "firsts" and to other claims about how great the college is. It is always useful to read these and to consider how persuaded you are that these claims make a college great. Personally, we are swept away sometimes by how impressive a college is, and sometimes we are not very impressed at all. It is worthwhile, though, to see how good a story a college can tell about itself when it tries really hard to do so.

One feature of many of these brag lists is **how highly ranked, nationally and even internationally, various academic departments are** (e.g., the ninth-best electrical engineering department in the U.S., in the top 20 departments of political science nationwide, etc.). You might not find these claims too interesting—unless you want to major in a department that is highly ranked. Some the most impressive departmental praise we ever read was this: **Rutgers, The State University of New Jersey**, claims to have one of the top three philosophy programs in the English-speaking world—along with New York University and the U.K.'s University of Oxford. We think that probably is worth bragging about.

And what about the rankings of colleges that are done by various well-known organizations and popular publications? If a college gets a high ranking on one list or another, it will usually publicize that ranking on its website. When looking at such rankings, remember that different ranking systems base their rankings on different factors—some of which might be of no interest at all to you. So look at rankings if you wish (because it is actually rather hard to ignore them), but **keep in mind that college rankings won't tell you how you will fit into that campus—academically or socially**. And it's that "fit" that will determine just how happy you will be.

> ✓ Go to **Question 2.** Jot down any "firsts," top-ranked departments, or other impressive claims about the college.

Type of College—Public or Private

By the time you have finished reading and jotting down the history of the college, you will know whether it is public, private nonprofit, public/private, or private for-profit. Here are some definitions:

- **Public colleges are paid for, in part, by state and local governments**—that means, by taxes. For this reason, they are understandably operated primarily for the benefit of their own residents. As a result, public colleges have reasonably low tuition for state and local residents, but nonresidents have to pay more.

    Even though public colleges are supported with tax dollars, they are not totally free to attend. Student tuition is still a major source of revenue for them. There has been a lot in the news recently as one state after another has raised the tuition at its public colleges, and that trend will likely continue.

    Each state has a public flagship university (as we described back in Step 1). Public flagship universities are not equally good or equally respected; some are much more attractive than others—both to students in their own states and to out-of-state students. Just to make it more complicated, the public flagship university in some states is actually a university "system," with a main campus (referred to as the flagship campus) plus regional campuses throughout the state (like **Penn State**). In those cases, the flagship campus is typically the most prestigious.

    Some states have more than one public system—like California, with its **University of California** campuses (the premier public system), its **California State University** campuses (the second tier of public colleges), and its **California Community Colleges System** campuses (the third tier of public colleges). When a state has more than one public system, make sure you understand which public system the college on your LLCO is part of. Pay attention to how selective and how widely respected that particular system is.

- **Private nonprofit colleges are funded by the tuition of their students and by donations** from their alumni/alumnae and others. Because private colleges typically have higher tuition rates than public colleges, the cost of attending a private college is likely to be higher than attending a public college.

    Of course, if a student is awarded a generous scholarship by a private college, that would bring tuition down—maybe to a public college level or maybe even lower. But, students can be awarded scholarships by public colleges, too, making the cost of attending a public college still more attractive.

- **Public-private partnerships are rare**, but here is a great example. On its Ithaca campus in upstate New

York, **Cornell University** offers a variety of schools/colleges to choose from at the undergraduate level—some private, some public. The private ones are the College of Architecture, Art, and Planning; the College of Arts and Sciences; the College of Engineering; and the School of Hotel Administration (which is now part of a newly formed College of Business). The public ones were established by an Act of the New York State Legislature and are funded, in part, by State money: the College of Agriculture and Life Sciences, the College of Human Ecology, and the School of Industrial and Labor Relations. A New York State resident attending any of the public ones would get an Ivy League education at a far more reasonable public price.

- **Private for-profit colleges**, sometimes called "proprietary colleges," are profit-making organizations, whose first responsibility is to their owners and stockholders rather than to their students. Proprietary colleges are in business to make money. Their business happens to be education. There is nothing necessarily wrong with that, but you should think about whether their motive to make money might affect their decisions about the resources they put into the education they provide. Remember that proprietary colleges are like private colleges when it comes to tuition. They are not cheap, and some do not have the scholarship funds available that both private and public colleges do.

    Some private for-profit colleges have been in the news lately as a result of students who have felt "ripped off" by a college that did not deliver the education it promised. We do not believe that all proprietary colleges provide a bad education; in fact, some provide a good education. But check carefully into the reputation of any private for-profit college you are interested in, and look for both a long history of success in educating students and plenty of satisfied graduates.

So which type of college is "best"? The fact is that **some private colleges are indeed better than some public colleges**; another fact is that **some public colleges are better than some private colleges**. By the time you finish your research for all of the colleges on your LLCO, you should be able to answer the question of which type or types of college are best for you.

> ✓ Go to **Question 3.** Check off the type of college—public, private nonprofit, public/private partnership, or private for-profit.

Special Mission of the College

By the time you have finished reading and jotting down the history of the college, you will also know whether the college was founded with any special mission and whether that mission continues today. Check specifically for these four missions, which might or might not be appealing to you:

- **Faith-based colleges and universities** include hundreds of small Bible colleges, which are dedicated to religious life and the study of religion, but also include very large universities that offer all fields of study, though with an underlying religious or moral or service-to-others orientation.

    Some faith-based institutions require more religious study than others. Some require students to take just a couple of courses in theology or perhaps philosophy, while others infuse much of their curriculum with their religious beliefs. Some require students to attend chapel services, but many do not.

    More U.S. colleges than you might think have been founded by religious denominations—including most of our earliest and most prestigious colleges. Some of them retain their religious affiliation today, but many do not.

    In our experience, **faith-based institutions are usually up front about what they are all about**. They are not trying to trick you into going there, because that wouldn't be good for you or for them. It is common for a faith-based institution to have a statement of its religious beliefs on its website, so look for it in your research. You can read it and see whether you and your family agree with it.

    Some faith-based institutions are Jewish, some are Catholic, and some are Protestant. One interesting choice is **Soka University of America** (SUA), located in Orange County, California: "Proudly founded upon the Buddhist principles of peace, human rights and the sanctity of life, SUA offers a non-sectarian curriculum" and welcomes students of all beliefs (quoted from its website).

    Understanding the world of some 200 Catholic colleges and universities in the U.S. is particularly complicated because they have been founded by various orders (including the Jesuits, Franciscans, Dominicans, and more) and by other groups within the Catholic community. Many respected Catholic institutions, including some of the best-known ones, attract many students who are not Catholic.

If you are researching the history of a faith-based institution, be sure to check out the faith-based part of its history, which might or might not be appealing to you. For example, the Jesuits, with their roots in Paris in the 1500s, trace their commitment to education to St. Ignatius of Loyola, who founded the first Jesuit college in Messina, Sicily, in 1548. Jesuit institutions today place a strong emphasis on intellectual rigor and a liberal arts foundation, social justice issues worldwide, and a life of service, as you will see on the website of any Jesuit college you research.

- **HBCUs** were established with the mission of educating African-American students. Today, there are just over 100 HBCUs, located in many states. They are public and private, large and small, faith-based and not, two-year and four-year colleges; some have graduate schools.

  HBCUs were founded to serve students who had been excluded from many other higher education institutions because of their race. The three earliest HBCUs were founded in Pennsylvania and Ohio before the Civil War, but many were founded in the South shortly after the Civil War. Those Southern HBCUs share a proud tradition of becoming the first collegiate homes of freed slaves and their family members.

  Today, some observers have said that it has become harder for HBCUs to recruit African-American students inasmuch as they are welcome at all colleges across the U.S.; however, enrollment has gone up at quite a few HBCUs recently. Interestingly, there has also been an increase in the number of Hispanic students enrolling at HBCUs.

  Without a doubt, **there is a strong sense of tradition on HBCU campuses and a strong sense of community and shared culture among the alumni/alumnae of HBCUs.**

- **HSIs**—that is, Hispanic-Serving Institutions—have been designated as such in just the past 50 years. By definition, HSIs have a student enrollment that is at least 25 percent Hispanic. For example, **The University of New Mexico** in Albuquerque, a federally designated HSI, was one of the first minority-majority universities, with a student body that was approximately 45 percent Hispanic and 35 percent Anglo.

  There are over 250 colleges and universities designated as HSIs, and they are located in states across the U.S. from California to Massachusetts and from Washington to Florida. Some HSIs are large public universities, some are large public community colleges, and some are small private liberal arts colleges. **Many HSIs receive federal funds to support programs and scholarships that are designed to help low-income Hispanic students succeed in college.**

  Although HSIs do not have the same kind of historical traditions that HBCUs have—perhaps because they were not originally founded with a mission to serve Hispanic students—they do offer a supportive environment, especially for first-generation-to-college Hispanic students.

- **Single-sex colleges and universities** enroll only women or only men and are all private institutions. Let's remember that the colleges and universities that were started in America's earliest days were all institutions enrolling only men. They were all single-sex institutions then.

  If you are researching the history of Ivy League schools, you will find that seven of the eight served only male students when they were founded in the 1600s and 1700s. (Only **Cornell University**, the youngest of the Ivies, was founded as a coeducational institution.) As time went on, many of the Ivies created a separate "sister" school for women: the **University of Pennsylvania** had its College for Women, **Columbia University** had Barnard, **Brown University** had Pembroke, and **Harvard University** had Radcliffe. Of these, only **Barnard College** remains as its own institution.

  Today, there are just over 40 women's colleges in the U.S., but only a handful of men's colleges. For whatever reason (probably financial), some of the women's colleges now allow men to enroll in their graduate programs or in special programs for returning adult students, thus maintaining the traditional women's college atmosphere only for their undergraduate residential students.

  If you are interested in a women's college, check out the Women's College Coalition website and the available downloadable guide *Why a Women's College?*

If you are interested in a men's college, check out **Morehouse College**, which is an academically rigorous HBCU located in Atlanta and which is the men's counterpart to **Spelman College**, a well-respected women's HBCU. Morehouse has a roster of famous alumni, ranging from Martin Luther King, Jr., to Samuel L. Jackson and Spike Lee—and that is quite a range. **Hampden-Sydney College** was founded in Virginia in 1775 and has a fascinating history (Patrick Henry and James Madison were among its first trustees). And there is **Wabash College**, located in Indiana and cited in the book *Colleges That Change Lives* as an institution that is particularly successful in creating engaged students, who go on to become leaders in their chosen fields.

As you do your research into colleges, you will find that, while most single-sex institutions have opened their doors to both men and women over the years and especially in the past 50 years, **those single-sex institutions that remain carry on a tradition that their graduates wholeheartedly support**. Many of their graduates believe that their students focus better on their studies in the classroom. Many of their graduates believe that their students develop a stronger sense of community and camaraderie with their classmates. Many of their graduates appreciate the histories and philosophies of their institutions—especially graduates of women's colleges, who feel that they are better supported as young women and are more encouraged to set and pursue whatever education and career goals they can imagine for themselves.

> ✓ Go to **Question 4.** Check off any special mission of the college.

STEP 5:
RESEARCH THE COLLEGE'S LOCATION

Step 5 focuses on college location. In the next section of the **College Profile Worksheet**, you will see **Questions 5, 6, and 7** on **Location**. All three can be answered easily from a college's website.

> ✓ Go to **Question 5**. Jot down the location (city and state) of the college.

You really should have known this already, without even having to look at the college website. Or, perhaps you knew the state, but not the city. We use the term "city" quite loosely, because many colleges are located in suburbs, small towns, and rural communities—and that brings us to the next question.

Type of Community

The type of community a college is located in might be very important to you and your parents, but for very different reasons. Some students can't wait to get away from the type of community they grew up in, while others can't imagine being comfortable in a new physical and cultural environment.

You need to know the community setting for each college on your LLCO so that you can decide whether the setting makes a difference to you. How will you think about that decision?

Are cities great? They are. Urban centers offer a general sense of excitement, along with many cultural opportunities (museums and theaters and concert halls and so on). They have ethnic, racial, and cultural diversity, which is a plus for many families. Many cities also have good public transportation, which is a plus for college students who don't have their own cars. Finally, many cities have more than one college (and some have a lot more than one college), which gives students an opportunity to meet all kinds of students and make all kinds of friends.

But are the suburbs great? They are, in a different way. Suburbs are relatively safe, for one thing, making them a good choice in the minds of lots of students (and lots of parents). They are also likely to be cheaper in terms of everyday living expenses, including movies, drug store items, groceries, and off-campus meals. They also might offer convenient commuter transportation options for getting into a nearby city, so that you can have the best of both worlds.

But are rural communities great? They are, again in a different way. Similar to suburbs, they are likely to be safe and low cost, when it comes to everyday spending. But, maybe more important for the students who are attracted to rural colleges, many rural communities offer a scenic and unspoiled environment, which lends itself to loads of outdoor sports and recreation, like hiking and biking.

But are small towns great? They are, too, in a still different way. Small towns are not really rural themselves, though they might be set in a rural area. They are not really suburban themselves, because they are not right outside a bigger city. And they are certainly not urban in terms of size, though they might have a substantial downtown, with cultural and social activities readily available. But, whatever they are, small towns are the locations of many of our nation's colleges. Many of these small towns are "great college towns," according to the students who go there and, interestingly enough, according to the people who live there.

Whether bright lights or forest glades are your thing, you can find a college there. So, where are your college options located?

> ✓ Go to **Question 6.** Check off the type of community the college is located in.

Information About the Community

We like to call this "cool stuff about the community." We can't tell you exactly what to look for here, but you will know it when you see it. In fact, as you do your research, you will see that **some college websites have whole sections devoted to talking about the community that surrounds the college**. For example, colleges in beautiful rural settings often talk about the nature walks, biking paths, hiking trails, waterfalls, lakes, forests, and so on that the college's students have easy access to.

Some colleges boast about their ranking on one list or another, like "the best college towns in America" or "the most affordable college towns," published by various magazines and college-oriented publications. *Travel + Leisure* magazine publishes such a list. *Forbes* magazine has its own method of calculating its list of best and worst college towns by using 23 academic, social, and financial measures. Some colleges will even reference the spots they earned on these lists in their *At a Glance* pages or in their lists of awards won.

What are some great college towns? In no particular order, here are a few named by various lists (you might want to find out what colleges are located there):

- College Station, TX
- Charlottesville, VA
- Saratoga Springs, NY
- Asheville, NC
- Flagstaff, AZ
- Boulder, CO
- Santa Cruz, CA
- St. Augustine, FL
- Burlington, VT
- Annapolis, MD
- Ann Arbor, MI
- Athens, GA
- Oxford, MS
- Iowa City, IA

There are plenty of lists you can look at, but you can also just read up on the community surrounding each college on your LLCO. While you probably shouldn't choose a college based on its surrounding community, some communities will be more attractive to you than others. So, it doesn't hurt to have the information available when deciding.

> ✓ Go to **Question 7.** Jot down information and advertising claims about the community and surrounding area, including natural beauty, historic sites, entertainment venues, restaurants, recreation opportunities, and so on.

STEP 6:
RESEARCH THE COLLEGE'S ENROLLMENT

Step 6 will help you find out everything you could ever want to know about the enrollment of the colleges on your LLCO. The **College Profile Worksheet** has nine questions about how many students are enrolled and what their personal characteristics are. While these questions can be answered from a college's website (especially by looking at the common data set), it is actually easier to get most of the answers by using College Navigator. So, start there to answer **Questions 8-16** on **Enrollment**.

Number of Undergraduate Students

Here is one very important thing to remember when you are jotting down undergraduate enrollment for each of the colleges on your LLCO: **Be consistent about what statistic you use.** For example, some colleges include part-time and full-time students in their enrollment count; others separate them. Sometimes, it is hard to know what students are included. Ideally, you should use numbers that mean the same thing from college to college so that you can compare the sizes of the undergraduate student body as accurately as possible.

Our vote for where to find that undergraduate enrollment number is College Navigator. After you search for your college, you will see many categories of data that are available. Click on *Enrollment*. You will refer to this category a lot as you fill out this section of the **College Profile Worksheet**.

Under *Enrollment*, you will notice that the figures are probably for the fall of the preceding school year. Those figures are fine to use, because most colleges do not have huge enrollment changes from year to year.

If your college has only undergraduate students (as with many small private liberal arts colleges), the heading will simply be *Total Enrollment (All Undergraduate)*. Use that number. If your college or university also has graduate students, the first line will be *Total Enrollment*, but *Undergraduate Enrollment* will be right beneath it. So, make sure that you use that undergraduate enrollment number.

> ✓ Go to **Question 8**. Jot down the undergraduate enrollment of the college.

Eventually, you will have to consider whether the size of the undergraduate student body matters to you. We think that this issue is given too much weight by many high school students and their parents. We often hear kids say things like this: "I think I would like to go to a small school. The University of *(fill in the blank)* seems too big to me." Of course, a big university might seem overwhelming to a high school senior. But perhaps that is because most high school seniors have spent no time at all in a large university setting. **We believe that most high school seniors have no rational basis for making a valid judgment about student body size.**

And, although it is tempting, we don't think you can judge the size of a college based on the size of your high school. If you are coming from a small public high school or a small private school, we understand that you might feel that you would get lost in the shuffle of a large university. We understand that, for you right now, a large academic setting might be outside your 17-year-old comfort zone. But that is no reason to assume that you would not do well in that larger academic setting, given half a chance a year from now.

As we move on, we want you to take a closer look at the students who make up that undergraduate enrollment—just in case what you find out would have any effect on your interest in the college or in your parents' interest in sending you there.

Breakdown by Full-Time and Part-Time Attendance

Is the breakdown of full-time *vs.* part-time undergraduate students something that you and your parents want to consider when choosing colleges to apply to? If so, let's find out what that breakdown is for colleges on your LLCO.

Stay in College Navigator in the *Enrollment* category. After the enrollment figures, you will see some pie graphs/pie charts/circle graphs. If your college has only undergraduate students, the first one will be called *Attendance Status*. The graph will show you the breakdown between full-time and part-time students in easy-to-see blue and yellow sections. If your college or university also has graduate students, the first graph will be *Undergraduate Attendance Status*. Either way, there's the answer to the next question on the worksheet.

> ✓ Go to **Question 9.** Jot down the breakdown of undergraduate students by full-time *vs.* part-time attendance.

Some colleges—especially prestigious private four-year colleges—have relatively few part-time students compared to, say, large public universities with many schools and many diverse programs. For example, in the fall of 2015, **Kenyon College** (a great private liberal arts college in Gambier, Ohio) had just 1 percent part-time undergraduate enrollment. On the other hand, **Kent State University** (a good public university, though not Ohio's flagship university) had 19 percent part-time undergraduate enrollment at its main campus in Kent, Ohio. Or, to take a different state, **Hunter College** (one of the best campuses of the public **City University of New York**) had 28 percent part-time undergraduate enrollment, while **New York University** (an excellent private university about 60 blocks away in Manhattan) had just 5 percent part-time undergraduate enrollment. You can see the differences, but do they matter to you?

Obviously, students could choose to study part time at a college for many reasons, including financial constraints, family responsibilities, and work obligations. Part-time students are not worse students; however, part-time students do likely lead fuller, more complicated, more off-campus lives than traditional freshmen enrolling right out of high school, especially if those freshmen are living on campus. As a result, **colleges with high part-time enrollment might have a bit of a different feel on campus compared to colleges where almost all of the students are there full time** (and, especially, where many of them are living on campus in residential housing). It's something to consider.

Breakdown by Gender

Unless you have been talking about going to a single-sex college, this statistic might not even be on your radar screen. Nonetheless, it might be something worth thinking about.

Stay in College Navigator in the *Enrollment* category. Next to the graph on attendance status is one that shows the male/female breakdown of undergraduate enrollment, again in easy-to-see blue and yellow sections. If your college has only undergraduate students, the graph will be *Student Gender*. If your college or university also has graduate students, the graph will be *Undergraduate Student Gender*. So, there's the answer to the next question on the worksheet.

> ✓ Go to **Question 10.** Jot down the breakdown of undergraduate students by gender.

If you look at the enrollment statistics for many colleges, you will notice that some are split pretty evenly between male and female students (say, 46 percent *vs.* 54 percent), while others are way out of balance (say, 30 percent *vs.* 70 percent). Sometimes colleges that are out of balance can be explained by their history (for example, they were once women's colleges) or by the types of majors they are best known for (given that some majors, unfortunately, continue to attract more students of one gender). If you want a college to reflect the general undergraduate college student population, it is interesting to note that **enrollment figures overall in the fall of 2014 showed that 56 percent of undergraduate students were female**. So, if a college is better balanced than that (in other words, closer to 50–50), it might well be working hard to achieve that balance

Let's look at a few examples. **Carleton College** (a great private liberal arts college in Northfield, Minnesota) is 53 percent female and 47 percent male. Carleton is working at it, we would say. Oddly enough, the gigantic **University of Minnesota** (the excellent public flagship university in the Twin Cities) gets even closer—at 51 percent female and 49 percent male. Not too far away, the **Milwaukee School of Engineering** (a Wisconsin college that specializes in engineering and technical subjects, though not exclusively) posts a 24 percent female and 76 percent male enrollment—for perhaps obvious reasons.

We should note here that we have not yet seen data reported and presented across colleges on enrollment of students with gender identities other than male and female. However, if you are looking for a college that is particularly accepting of more diverse gender identities, that is a topic that can and should be pursued by looking further on the college's website and by calling the Admission Office and asking about relevant data and policies.

> ✓ Stay in **Question 10**. Jot down any gender identity information or policies you find on the college website or in discussion with the Admission Office.

Breakdown by Race/Ethnicity

Unless you have been talking about going to an HBCU or about seeking out an HSI, you might not have been thinking hard about the racial or ethnic background of students at the colleges on your LLCO. But it might be something worth considering, depending on your comfort level with members of other racial and ethnic groups in an education setting. For example, if you attend a racially and ethnically mixed high school, you would likely feel comfortable in a similar sort of college population. However, if you attend a high school that is not racially and ethnically diverse, it might be even more important to find a college that is—in order to prepare yourself better for the world of work and for life.

We have talked about the racial and ethnic diversity of colleges in our podcast episodes, and we noted that some colleges are not nearly as diverse as we would have guessed they were. For example, we looked at a geographically diverse sample of nine large and small public flagships, some highly selective and others less selective. The percentage of black students ranged from just 2 percent to 15 percent. The Hispanic/Latino numbers ranged from just 3 percent to 10 percent.

On the other hand, **we know quite a few very selective private colleges and universities where the percentages of black and Hispanic/Latino students exceed these public university numbers**. That is worth thinking about—whether you are black or Hispanic/Latino yourself or whether you simply want to attend a college with a diverse student population.

So, stay in College Navigator in the *Enrollment* category. Under the graphs on attendance status and student gender is a bar graph that shows the racial/ethnic breakdown of undergraduate enrollment into nine categories (we will have you look at only the first eight categories). If your college has only undergraduate students, the bar graph will be entitled *Student Race/Ethnicity*. If your college or university also has graduate students, the bar graph will be entitled *Undergraduate Race/Ethnicity*. Either way, there's the answer to the next question on the worksheet.

> ✓ Go to **Question 11**. Jot down the breakdown of undergraduate students by race/ethnicity.

Breakdown by Student Residence

It is useful, we think, to see just how many undergraduate students at a college are from the state where that college is located. Generally, we believe it is better to go to a college where you will meet students from all over—all over the U.S., but also from all over the world. Living and working with students of many national backgrounds in a relatively safe and protected environment, like a college, is one way for you to gain the interpersonal skills you will need for a lifetime.

As we have said before, almost all colleges like the idea of having students from all over the country and, indeed, from all over the world. Many, many colleges proudly say on their websites how many states and how many foreign countries their students come from. While public universities have a duty to serve the students of their own state, even they like to draw students from other states and other countries. And remember that **you might get into a college far away from home that your grades and test scores and activities could not get you into close to home**—because, for that faraway college, you bring desirable geographic diversity. Think about that.

So, stay in College Navigator in the *Enrollment* category. Under the graph on race/ethnicity is a bar graph that shows the residences of undergraduate students in four categories (we will have you look at only the first three categories). It is called *Undergraduate Student Residence*. So, there's the answer to the next question on the worksheet.

> ✓ Go to **Question 12.** Jot down the breakdown of undergraduate students by student residence.

Let's look at a few public university examples. In the fall of 2015, the **University of Alaska** at its flagship campus in Fairbanks enrolled 90 percent in-state students (for reasons you might guess), 9 percent out-of-state students, and 1 percent foreign students. The **University of Washington** at its flagship campus in Seattle enrolled 66 percent in-state students, 18 percent out-of-state students, and 15 percent foreign students. But the **University of New Hampshire** at its flagship campus in Durham actually enrolled just 41 percent in-state students, 58 percent out-of-state students, and 1 percent foreign students. Just from these three examples, you can see how different the make-up of public flagship universities can be when it comes to where they get their students.

In case you are wondering, a college's own website will often break down enrollment even further than College Navigator to give you additional facts, like the five states sending the most undergraduate students or the most new freshmen or the percent of students who come from neighboring states or who come from the region the college is located in. All of that might be food for thought as you review colleges on your LLCO.

> ✓ Stay in **Question 12.** Jot down any other interesting facts you find on the college website about where its students come from.

Support Services

While support services—like academic advising, personal counseling, and employment assistance—can be useful to any undergraduate student, these support services are often particularly important to groups of students who might find it more difficult to adjust to college life, either socially or academically, especially when they find themselves in the minority of students on a college campus.

If you identify with students of color, first-generation-to-college students, LGBTQ students, students with learning disabilities, or another group, you should take a look at whether each college on your LLCO has support services targeted for you. For example, **Georgia State University** has an impressive Office of Black Student Achievement, which provides a wide variety of academic, support, leadership, and outreach activities, programs, and services. That says something about its commitment to serving its black student population.

When you are looking for support services like that on a college's website, see whether you can find any evidence that the services provided are actually successful. Why? Because **successful support services can make all the difference between dropping out and graduating**.

> ✓ Go to **Question 13.** Jot down any interesting information you find about support services targeted for particular groups of students, especially if you are a member of that group.

Retention Rate

Retention rate tells you what percent of freshmen come back to the college the next year as sophomores. In other words, **it tells you how well the college keeps its students coming back for more**.

There are many reasons that kids leave college between their first and second years, and some of those reasons are certainly beyond a college's control. Nonetheless, you probably want to be looking for colleges with a high retention rate—at least 80 percent or better. Many top-ranked colleges will post a retention rate above 90 percent.

So, stay in College Navigator, but move to the *Retention and Graduation Rates* category. Under the first heading, *First-to-Second Year Retention Rates*, there is a bar graph entitled *Retention Rates for First-Time Students Pursuing Bachelor's Degrees*. This is what you are, assuming you are headed to a four-year college. You want to look at the bar for full-time students (some colleges also have a bar for part-time students). So, there's the answer to the next question on the worksheet.

> ✓ Go to **Question 14.** Jot down the retention rate for full-time students who returned to the college for a second year.

Graduation Rates

Graduation rate is exactly what you think—the percent of students who actually graduated from the college. But there is a lot more detail available in College Navigator than you will ever need to know.

Stay in the *Retention and Graduation Rates* category. Under the third heading, *Bachelor's Degree Graduation Rates*, there is a bar graph entitled *Graduation Rates for Students Pursuing Bachelor's Degrees*. There are double bars for 4-year, 6-year, and 8-year graduation rates. The yellow and blue bars simply stand for two different entering classes of freshmen. You want to check out the 4-year graduation rate and, reluctantly, the 6-year graduation rate.

Obviously, **we all hope that you will get out of college four years after you start, even though many students don't do that anymore**. We hope that, and you probably hope that. But your parents really hope that. Not getting out in four years will run up your college costs even higher than they are already going to be. You need to stay focused and get out of college in four years.

The higher the 4-year graduation rates are, the better. Rates over 80 percent are good, though they might be lower in big universities, especially public ones. So, judge accordingly.

> ✓ Go to **Question 15.** Jot down the 4-year and 6-year graduation rates for students pursuing bachelor's degrees.

Graduate Enrollment

Whether a college (or, more often, a university) has graduate students at all is an important aspect of choosing a college for some students. **Some students and parents like the idea of advanced scholarship being available on campus and of professional schools (like law and medicine and journalism) being right there, too**—either to add prestige generally or to serve as motivation or even the next stop for a successful undergrad. On the other hand, some parents and even some college professors think that graduate students distract a college from paying adequate attention to the needs and education of the undergraduates; they also feel that too many graduate students (rather than college professors) end up teaching the freshman-level courses in too many disciplines.

Whichever way you think about it, knowing whether there are graduate students at a college and how many of them there are is one reasonable thing to consider in choosing colleges to apply to.

Stay in College Navigator and go back to the *Enrollment* category. If your college or university has graduate students, the first line will be *Total Enrollment*, and *Graduate Enrollment* will be listed underneath it. So, there's the answer to the final question on enrollment on the worksheet.

> ✓ **Go to Question 16. Jot down the graduate enrollment of the college.**

STEP 7:
RESEARCH THE COLLEGE'S CLASS SIZE

Step 7 asks you to consider class size as one indication of what your academic experience would be like at each college on your LLCO. In other words, we want you to look at how undergraduate enrollment is distributed into the actual classrooms and seminar rooms and labs that you will sit in on campus and how that might affect your relationships with your professors. The **College Profile Worksheet** has just two questions in this section. You will need to use both College Navigator and each college's website to find the answers to **Questions 17 and 18** on **Class Size**.

For the record, we understand that some undergraduates will take one or more online courses or blended courses (partly online, partly in a classroom) during their undergraduate years. This section of the worksheet, however, focuses on class size for those courses that are taken in an actual classroom.

Student-to-Faculty Ratio

You should look to College Navigator to find the student-to-faculty ratio for each college—in other words, how many students are there for each faculty member. This is a statistic that we mentioned frequently during our virtual college tour, and we know that it is one that many colleges themselves are very proud of. That's why it is often included in advertising claims about a college.

While you can usually find this statistic on a college's own website—typically on the *Quick Facts* or *At a Glance* or similar page—you can also spend lots of time looking for this statistic and NOT finding it on the website. Trust us on that! So, it's quicker to use College Navigator, which presents a college's undergraduate student-to-faculty ratio on the last line of the opening section of each college's profile.

> ✓ Go to **Question 17.** Jot down the student-to-faculty ratio of the college.

So, what is the big deal about student-to-faculty ratio? It is simply this: **Most people believe that a student's education is improved if he or she has more access to faculty members**—in smaller classes, during less crowded office hours, and through a variety of activities, such as mentorships, special lectures, and so on. Most people believe that faculty members can and will give each student enough time and attention if they are not spread too thin over too many students. Hence, a student-to-faculty ratio should be as low as possible, ideally in single digits or low double digits—like 10-to-1, or 10 students to each faculty member.

We actually don't have any evidence that this is true, though it certainly seems to be logical. We also don't know how valuable a low student-to-faculty ratio is for students who are not particularly looking for this kind of personal relationship with faculty members. Many students attend large universities, have relatively little one-to-one contact with their professors, and still get an excellent education. As a matter of fact, some students actually prefer that.

Nonetheless, if you think that you would benefit from a closer, perhaps more nurturing connection to your professors, then checking out the student-to-faculty ratio makes sense. Or, if your parents would feel better knowing that there is a greater chance that a faculty member knows you and is looking out for you, then searching out that low student-to-faculty ratio is important.

Generally speaking, student-to-faculty ratios are lower at small private colleges than at large public universities, which is not surprising. Small private colleges advertise the college culture that comes with a low ratio as one of the reasons to choose a small private college instead of a large public university. For example, you have **Amherst College** at 8-to-1, **Vassar College** at 8-to-1, **Reed College** at 9-to-1, **Hamilton College** at 9-to-1, **Colorado College** at 10-to-1, and so on. If you look at a list of good public flagship universities, those ratios might be more like 16- or 17- or 18-to-1.

When you see a very selective private university with a student-to-faculty ratio that makes it look more like a small private college, you have to be impressed—like **Rice University** at 6-to-1 or **Duke University** at 7-to-1. Though perhaps the most interesting is **California Institute of Technology** (commonly known as Caltech), with a student-to-faculty ratio of 3-to-1—a ratio so low that it is almost literally incredible. A low ratio like one of these might make a private university a more attractive choice to you, but probably a more expensive choice, too.

One word of caution: It is possible, even likely, that these ratios are not calculated exactly the same way from college to college, regardless of what anyone claims. It is also likely that the ratio is a lot harder to calculate for a large university with, say, 12 schools and colleges in it, which could have different student-to-faculty ratios; in that case, one student-to-faculty ratio doesn't even make much sense. In fairness to College Navigator, colleges do get directions for completing the standard data collection forms. For example, student-to-faculty ratio is supposed to exclude both students and faculty in what we would think of as professional programs that are solely for graduate students—like medicine, law, social work, or public health. So, College Navigator is doing its best to make the ratios meaningful and comparable from college to college.

The bottom line is this: Don't think much about the difference between a student-to-faculty ratio of, say, 9-to-1 and 10-to-1 or even 11-to-1. Instead, **consider that there might be a difference in faculty accessibility between a college with a student-to-faculty ratio of 9-to-1 and one with a ratio of 18-to-1**.

Class Size

Class size is exactly what you think it is—how many students are in the classroom with you when you are trying to learn calculus or French literature or whatever you are taking. Some colleges are very proud of their small class sizes. **Other colleges that think they don't have very much to be proud of regarding class size do the best they can to make a good case for their own class sizes.** You can find this information on many, many college websites, though you might have to look around a bit. Happy hunting!

For example, here is what you will read under *Quick Facts* on the website for **St. John's College**: "Seminars have between 17 [and] 19 students, led by two faculty members. Tutorials (mathematics, language, and music) and laboratory sessions have 12 to 16 students, led by one faculty member." That is believable, given that St. John's (with campuses in Annapolis and Santa Fe) is an extremely small and super-intriguing college (with about 450 to 475 students on each campus). St. John's classes are a lot smaller than many classes would be at a large university.

On the website of the **College of William & Mary** (a prestigious public college of about 6,300 undergraduates and 2,200 graduate students in Williamsburg, Virginia), you will find this statement under *W&M At a Glance*: "84 percent of courses have fewer than 40 students." Clearly, William & Mary thinks that is worth advertising, though you can see that it is quite different from what St. John's advertises.

Or you can search for the common data set on college websites and check out a display of class section sizes under *I. Instructional Faculty and Class Size* (by the way, you will also find student-to-faculty ratios here). You can see how many class sections have 2-9 students, 10-19 students, 20-29 students, 30-39 students, and all the way to 100+ students. There are also "subsection" sizes displayed—that is, supplementary tutorials and labs, for example.

But again, class size is a matter of personal choice—at least it is once you get into college and take a variety of courses so you know what you are talking about. Some students prefer large classes, like a huge lecture by a brilliant professor. Other students prefer small seminars where students get to express their own opinions and talk back and forth with each other and with the professor. Our honest opinion is that you can't possibly know right now which of these you would prefer. Why? Because you, like most high school students, have never experienced huge lectures by brilliant professors. Are we right?

> ✓ **Go to Question 18.** Jot down any information and advertising claims made about class size.

STEP 8: RESEARCH THE COLLEGE'S ACADEMICS

Step 8 is what college is all about—or, at least, mainly about. The **College Profile Worksheet** has six questions in this section, and they cover a lot of ground. You will need to go to each college's website to find the answers to **Questions 19-24** on **Academics**.

Schools and Colleges

As you know by now, universities and large institutes (like **Massachusetts Institute of Technology**) are made up of schools and/or colleges that focus on different disciplines. Some of these institutions are composed of a small number of schools/colleges (say, four or five), but some are composed of quite a large number (as many as 15 or more). Some schools/colleges are only for graduate or professional students, who already have a bachelor's degree; examples of these are law, medicine, dentistry, and veterinary medicine. Some schools/colleges within a university or institute are only for undergraduate students. And some schools/colleges within a university or institute serve both undergraduate and graduate students. You have to do some careful reading when researching which are which, but you will find all of them listed in the *Academics* section of a college's website.

By the time you answer this question for five or six institutions, you will see that lots of their colleges/schools have the same name, like Business, Management, Education, Health Care, Social Work, Journalism, Engineering, and Architecture. Some have quite similar names, like various versions of Arts and Sciences for the liberal arts and sciences school that virtually all large institutions have. But some have really novel and interesting names, too— Travel Industry Management, Ocean & Earth Science & Technology, Pacific & Asian Studies, Tropical Agriculture & Human Resources, and Hawaiʻinuiākea School of Hawaiian Knowledge (just some of the 15 schools/colleges at the public flagship **University of Hawaiʻi at Mānoa**).

You will need to figure out which school/college you are most interested in applying to because many institutions will not let you apply to more than one school/college within the institution. Think hard about that right now, while you are taking the time to read about all of them.

> ✓ Go to **Question 19**. Jot down the schools/colleges within any institution you are researching. Check off the ones that serve undergraduate students. Double check the one that you are most interested in.

Academic Departments

Now, you need to go one step further and research the academic departments at the institution. Universities obviously have more departments across all of its schools/colleges than smaller liberal arts colleges have. There is often an alphabetical listing of all of the departments in the *Academics* section of a college's website.

You can't possibly write them all down and don't need to. Just start focusing on the ones that interest you most. Even if you are not sure what you want to study in college, **you will need to narrow the field in order to complete most college applications.**

> ✓ Go to **Question 20.** Jot down at least several academic departments that you are interested in.

Majors

And you are going to need to go still further and research the majors in one or more of the departments you chose when answering the previous question.

We know that this seems like a lot of detail if you are not at all sure what you want to study. **Unfortunately, many college applications will ask you to specify a major.** Some applications will also ask you to specify a second choice and even a third choice for a major. We say "unfortunately" because we know that many high school students are not ready to make this decision yet. We also know that many college students change their minds after they choose a major—even after a couple of college semesters. All that is to be expected from college freshmen and sophomores.

Nonetheless, you are likely to have to make a tentative decision about a major in order to complete at least some of your college applications. So, now is the time to start that research.

> ✓ Go to **Question 21.** Jot down at least several majors that you are interested in.

Getting a head start on thinking about majors will also give you a chance to talk to your high school teachers about your choices. For example, those of you who imagine majoring in biology and going to medical school eventually will notice that large universities have many majors within the Biology Department. **If you can't figure out which exact major(s) would be right for you, you won't make a convincing case for yourself in your application.**

Core Curriculum

For the purpose of this discussion, we will refer to this centuries-old curriculum concept as a **"core curriculum,"** though you might hear it referred to as a **"general education curriculum"** or as **"distribution requirements."** What it means is that all students in a college or in a specific college/school within a larger university or institute are usually required to take one or two courses in each of a broad range of academic disciplines, such as mathematics, or in each of a broad range of groups of disciplines, such as natural sciences, languages and literature, social sciences, and so on. Each college seems to have its own unique way of defining core requirements, and some definitions are more understandable than others.

Some colleges have quite strict requirements, meaning that there are many different requirements that have to be met, which might add up to 10 or more courses before it's all over. Some colleges have far fewer requirements for either the number of courses or the exact courses that have to be taken. And some colleges have no core curriculum at all. Would the presence of core curriculum requirements make a difference to you in choosing a college?

Let's take a moment to reflect on the purpose of a core curriculum. The concept comes from the liberal arts tradition, where students are supposed to be well rounded in their studies and in their understanding of the intellectual content and issues raised in many fields. **People in favor of this tradition would say that students do not know exactly where their careers and lives will take them and that the ability to solve problems and think critically across a range of academic subjects could make a difference in how well they succeed** in their careers (likely in their multiple careers) and indeed in their lives. It is no surprise that many liberal arts colleges as well as the arts and sciences college/school within many large institutions would require and proudly support a core curriculum for its students.

However, some non-liberal-arts colleges/schools within large universities also have instituted a core curriculum. One great example of this is the Fu Foundation School of Engineering and Applied Science at **Columbia University**, which has this impressive and perhaps surprising statement on its website:

> "Engineering has been called the newest liberal art. At Columbia Engineering, students not only study science and mathematics and gain technical skills but also study literature, philosophy, art history, music theory, and major civilizations through the Core Curriculum in the humanities. . . . Students are encouraged to consider the wide range of possibilities open to them, both academically and professionally. To this end, the first and second years of the four-year undergraduate program comprise approximately 66 semester points of credit that expose students to a cross-fertilization of ideas from different disciplines within the University." (quoted from the website)

So, at Fu, students are required to take quite a few liberal arts courses early on in their engineering program in order to provide some humanities balance to the heavy load of mathematics and sciences that all engineering students focus on. The brilliance of this position comes in the notion that students who find that engineering is not what they had expected are well equipped to transfer to another field of study and move many of those core credits with them. For some engineering students, these liberal arts courses might be a drag; for other engineering students, they might turn out to save the day.

Another advantage of a core curriculum is that it causes students to look into academic fields that are rarely taught in high schools—like anthropology or sociology or art history or linguistics. Without requirements in a variety of academic fields or groups of fields, many students would never take a look at some of these fields and would never know what they had missed.

Now, let's talk about those colleges that go one step further and require certain courses of all students—the actual courses, not just a number of courses in certain academic fields. So, instead of saying to students that they must take two courses in languages and literature, for example, the college will specify that all students must take Writing 101 and Public Speaking 101. **When a college decides to require specific courses, it is because its professors feel that those courses are most critical to developing the foundation for more advanced college study and/or to developing a broad understanding of and ability to engage in the modern world.** Because all students have taken these same required core courses, professors can use that shared knowledge to help students make connections across subject fields every year from then on.

In our virtual college tour, we often talked about the core curriculum requirements of a college. We did that for two reasons. First, we were truly impressed with some of them, even though we could tell that they would be quite challenging for students. Second, we knew that some students would love the idea of a core curriculum, while other students would hate it.

There are two groups of students who are likely to hate the idea the most. One group is students who do not feel confident in a range of academic fields (this often comes in the form of "I'd like to go to a college where I don't have to take any math"). The other group is students who are anxious to get on with what they already know they want to study and don't want to waste time with other things (this often comes in the form of "I want to be a mechanical engineer, and I don't see a need for these humanities requirements"). Are you in one of these groups?

Here is one intriguing example of a core curriculum. **St. John's College** (remember, with campuses in Annapolis and in Santa Fe) has a unique core liberal arts curriculum. It is based on collaborative inquiry in small class discussions, with the professor acting as a tutor and mentor—all based on the original texts of great authors in almost every subject field. The Seminar, as St. John's calls it, is the foundation for the curriculum, and it is described this way on the website:

> "Students participate in far-reaching and free but disciplined conversations about major works of literature, philosophy, political theory, theology, history, economics, and psychology from Homer and the Greek historians, playwrights, and philosophers in the freshman year, through the Renaissance in the sophomore year and the Enlightenment in the junior year, to the contemporary world in the senior year." (quoted from the website)

Students at St. John's are also required to take four years of mathematics, three years of laboratory science, two years of music (including singing in the Freshman Chorus together), and four years of a second language (two years of Ancient Greek and two years of modern French). Clearly, this is one serious set of core curriculum requirements.

While there are many colleges that have a core curriculum, as you will find in your research, let's take a look at just two examples of colleges that do NOT have one:

- At **The Evergreen State College**, a public liberal arts college in Washington's capital city of Olympia, students take one interdisciplinary course (called a "program") at a time. It might last one, two, or even three quarters. A program integrates several subjects and is taught by a team of professors from different subject fields. This is an intriguing and innovative approach to college. There are no required programs and no distribution requirements and no major requirements (because there are no majors) for earning a Bachelor of Arts degree.

- **Pitzer College**—one of the five undergraduate colleges in **The Claremont Colleges**, a highly respected consortium in California—offers its 1,000 students about 40 fields of study in an "interdisciplinary liberal arts education emphasizing social justice, intercultural understanding and environmental sensitivity" (quoted from the website). Students are expected to engage in community service and are given the freedom to create their own academic programs. There are no traditional core curriculum requirements.

So, get busy researching this topic. When the time comes to decide which colleges you will apply to, the number and rigor and comprehensiveness of any core curriculum requirements might well be something you will want to consider.

> ✓ Go to **Question 22**. Check off whether the college has a core curriculum. If it does, jot down the exact requirements listed on the website—whether they are specific courses, or a number of courses in specific academic subjects (e.g., mathematics), or a number of courses in groups of academic subjects (e.g., natural sciences, humanities), or all three.

Study Abroad Options

As we said earlier, study abroad options are not just for rich kids studying a foreign language anymore. Students who are from all kinds of backgrounds and who are studying all kinds of things are taking time to go to a different country to live and to learn. When you were making your LLCO, we suggested that you put one college outside the U.S. on your list. We were serious about that. By the way, you are likely to find that the college you picked is actually cheaper to attend than a private college here in the U.S., and you will see that many colleges offer degree programs taught in English. Surprising, isn't it?

But, for those of you who don't want to go to a college for four years in another country, take a close look at the study abroad options available at each college on your LLCO. These days, **many colleges have fantastic study abroad programs, which make it logistically easy for you to study outside the U.S.** These programs are already carefully set up, and they offer housing and other support while you are there. Some colleges have their own campuses in foreign countries, while others partner with a foreign university.

Some colleges strongly encourage their students to take a semester abroad; for example, at **Centre College**, a small liberal arts college in Kentucky, about 85 percent of students study abroad at least once and about 25 percent at least twice. And **a few colleges even require their students to study abroad**; for example, **Goucher College**, a small liberal arts college in Maryland, has been doing that since 2006 and now offers 60 programs in 32 foreign countries.

> ✓ Go to **Question 23**. Jot down the study abroad options that the college offers—both locations and programs. Include any important details.

For future reference, if a college you love doesn't have its own study abroad program, don't forget about what the American Institute for Foreign Study (AIFS) has to offer. Based in Stamford, Connecticut, AIFS operates a wide range of outstanding summer, semester-long, and year-long programs in over 20 countries on five continents.

In AIFS programs, students take college courses taught in English and receive college credits, which can be transferred back to the student's own college. If a student chooses to attend a program in a non-English-speaking country, then language courses are usually required. For example, in just a one-semester program, which opens with an intensive full-time two-week language course before the semester starts and continues with regular language classes during the semester, students can earn a full year of foreign language credits, which many liberal arts students need in order to fulfill bachelor's degree requirements. All of our firsthand experiences with AIFS have been fantastic.

You might not think that study abroad is something you are interested in right now, but you might change your mind when you see your friends going off to do it. We have no doubt that it could change your life.

Grading Practices

We bet that grading practices are not something most students consider before choosing a college—perhaps because they assume that colleges are quite traditional when it comes to awarding final course grades. Most colleges do, in fact, use some kind of numerical scale (typically, with a 4.0 as an A) or letter scale (typically, from A though F). These traditional grading practices might seem just fine to you.

However, **there are some colleges that are anything but traditional when it comes to evaluating student progress**. For example, take **Hampshire College** (an excellent and innovative private college in Amherst, Massachusetts), where students receive written narrative evaluations from professors on their assignments and as their final course grades. No numbers and no letters! Or, take **Bennington College** (a great private college in Bennington, Vermont), where students receive narrative evaluations at the end of each course, but may request letter grades; students interested in graduate school are encouraged to request letter grades for at least two years so that a GPA can be calculated for their graduate school applications.

Colleges that use narrative evaluations instead of traditional grades praise their value in teaching their students more about their own strengths and weaknesses, in getting their students to focus on their learning instead of on their grades, and in building better and more stimulating relationships between their students and their professors. That's probably something you never thought about before.

> ✓ **Go to Question 24.** Check off whether the college has a traditional grading system. If it does NOT, jot down the way that student work is evaluated instead.

STEP 9:
RESEARCH THE COLLEGE'S SCHEDULE

Step 9 looks at the components that make up the college schedule. For many colleges, these questions will produce a rather traditional response, something like this: a fall semester and a spring semester, each running about 15 weeks. There will also be a summer term or two, and there might even be a super-short winter term between the regular terms. But there are also innovative scheduling options that you probably never heard of and that you might find attractive. You will need to go to each college's website to research this topic and answer **Questions 25, 26, and 27** on **Schedule**.

Term Length and Course Length

Some students like to study something over many weeks because that allows them time for calm reflection and for breaks every once in a while. Other students like to study something over a shorter time period because that keeps them better engaged and focused and allows less time for forgetting. Some students can do very well when asked to concentrate on subjects or projects intensively in short bursts, but have trouble sustaining interest and attention over longer time frames. Other students are just the opposite.

Whatever your preference is, there is a college for you. You might not want to make college schedule the main reason for choosing a college, but you might find that it contributes to your thinking about how successful and comfortable you might be at a particular college. On the other hand, you might find a college schedule so intriguing that the schedule alone could push a college to the top of your list of options.

Many colleges operate on a traditional fall and spring semester system, with each semester's lasting from 15 to 18 weeks, depending how you count exam and holiday weeks. There are two semesters each year, and you attend both and take the summer off.

However, **Sterling College** (a fascinating private college in Craftsbury Common, Vermont) operates three full semesters per year—fall, spring, and summer. Students may attend all three (and finish college quicker) rather than just the traditional two per year. Student applications are reviewed on a rolling basis, and students may enter Sterling at any one of the three semesters.

Some colleges operate on a trimester system (three terms a year) **or a quarter system** (four terms a year), and each college determines how long the terms run and how many you attend in a year. For example, some colleges that operate on a quarter system run those quarters for 10 weeks each, but some trimester colleges also use 10-week terms. You simply have to look at what each college writes about its own schedule on its own website.

For example, **Carleton College** (an excellent private college in Northfield, Minnesota) operates on a trimester schedule of three 10-week terms, with students taking just three courses at a time, rather than the typical four or five courses that students take in most semester plans. Carleton's schedule of fewer courses at a time allows for the in-depth thinking that the college prides itself on having students do.

Looking again at **Bennington College**, some courses run three weeks, some seven weeks, and some the full 14 weeks each term, with course credits assigned accordingly. Bennington's schedule provides something for everyone and allows for lots of variety during the semester as courses begin and end.

> ✓ Go to **Questions 25 and 26**. Jot down how many weeks courses last, and remember that there might be more than one answer to that. Then, check off whether the college uses semesters, trimesters, quarters, or something else.

Innovative Options

Some colleges think way outside the scheduling box and come up with a plan that is completely different from semesters, trimesters, or quarters. If you have a college like that on your LLCO, you will want to think hard about how appealing its unusual schedule is to you.

For example, **Colorado College** (a great private college in Colorado Springs) has a unique Block Plan, **where students take all of their courses on a one-at-a-time schedule**, with each course about three and a half weeks long and taught typically from 9:00 a.m. to noon each weekday. At the end of each block, there is a four-day break so that students can relax and enjoy the natural beauty of Colorado's mountains and forests and canyons. Each block is the equivalent of one college course; students take four blocks per semester, or eight blocks per year, or 32 blocks during their time at the College. Frankly, we find this schedule totally persuasive and wildly appealing, but would you?

> ✓ Go to **Question 27**. Jot down the details of any truly innovative schedule you find.

Quite different and innovative scheduling options come from universities that want to make room for significant **cooperative (co-op) work experiences—meaning that students study full time in most terms, but then work full time in one or more terms in order to gain important job experience**. For example, at **Drexel University** (a good urban university in Philadelphia), students study in short 10-week quarters so that it is easier to work with employers to schedule the co-op work experiences. Students complete up to three co-op experiences during their time at Drexel; each one lasts about six months, and the average salary that students earn in each co-op experience is about $16,000. Wow! Similarly, about 90 percent of students at **Northeastern University** (a good urban university in Boston) complete at least one six-month co-op work experience in a career-related field; many Northeastern students complete two, and some even stay a fifth year to complete a third co-op work experience. They are that good.

STEP 10:
RESEARCH THE COLLEGE'S HOUSING

Step 10 calls for you to investigate on-campus housing options, which could make some difference to you if you were planning to live in college housing. Some of you will be commuting to campus, so these questions will seem less important to you; however, your plans could change before you start college or after you are enrolled, so housing is still worth a look—both freshman housing and upperclassman housing.

You will find in your research that there are some colleges where students live in campus housing well past the freshman year. Take **Hamilton College** (in Clinton, New York), where all students live on campus in 27 residence halls, or **St. Michael's College** (in Colchester, Vermont), where all full-time undergrads live on campus all four years unless they are living at home with family. Or look again at **Colorado College**, where there is a three-year on-campus housing requirement (with a few exceptions), or the **University of Rochester** in New York, where more than 90 percent of students live in campus housing. What are all those colleges—and their students—thinking? Of course, you will need to go to each college's website to research this topic and find out the answers to **Questions 28-31** on **Housing**.

Freshman Housing Requirement

Let us start by saying that **we think you should live on campus as a freshman if at all possible**, given whatever financial constraints your family has. As a matter of fact, many colleges actually require it—for both good and not-so-good reasons.

A really good reason is that living together in campus housing (whether that means traditional dorms or residential "houses" or something else) does promote a kind of camaraderie among students that is hard to develop any other way. **Living in close proximity to others in your same situation often provides a system of support and friendship that many kids at college want and need**—whether that comes from studying late into the evening/morning together or eating together or walking back and forth to classes together or meeting each other's friends and just hanging out together. Perhaps a not-so-good reason, though an understandable one from a college's point of view, is that colleges need to fill those dorm rooms and bring in the revenue that comes from filling them.

The importance of living on campus is similar to the importance of going away to college, in our opinion. Both provide you with a way to spread your wings in a relatively safe and protected environment before you are ready to be completely on your own. Living in campus housing requires you to figure out how to eat, study, do laundry, clean up, sleep enough, and manage money—without having to deal with the safety and transportation and utilities issues that come with off-campus housing and without the comparative ease of living at home.

So, even if you are going to a college in your hometown or within commuting distance of home, try to live on campus—especially if you can afford it, but even if you need to use scholarship funds or loans to cover it. Why? Because it is an integral part of the college experience—especially if you are attending a college close to home.

> ✓ Go to **Question 28**. Check off whether freshmen are required to live in on-campus residential housing.

Types of College Housing

Not all residential facilities are equally good when it comes to comfort, convenience, supervision, and security. Therefore, when choosing colleges to apply to, **remember to think about what residential life will be like not only when you are a freshman, but also when you are an upperclassman with different housing options**, including apartments off campus and perhaps fraternity and sorority houses.

The residential facilities that a college provides are usually well described—even bragged about—on a college's website, can be seen on virtual campus tours on the website, or can certainly be seen firsthand on a college visit. College tours love to take visiting kids and parents to look at dorms, even when they are of the most ordinary kind. While we don't think you should choose a college because of its housing facilities, we do think you might put housing in the scale when you are weighing your choices, which might mean taking a college off your LLCO if the housing options seem terrible.

Here are the housing options you are most likely to find in your research:

- **Many colleges have traditional college dorms**, with long halls of double and single rooms and a huge bathroom shared by everyone on the hall. There are usually upperclassmen serving as residential advisors—maybe one on each floor—who provide some level of supervision and support for students.

- **Many colleges have apartment-style suites**, with several bedrooms and a bathroom—and sometimes with a living area and a kitchen—for four to six or so students. Students in these suites often develop strong friendships, meaning that they take care of each other and watch out for each other. And there is still usually a residential advisor nearby.

- **Some colleges have really interesting residential houses**, which sponsor both social and academic activities for residents, often have one or two faculty families living with the students, often have their own eating facilities where everyone dines together, and have their own sense of community pride. And, clearly, the idea of some live-in adult supervision can be pretty appealing to your parents.

    For example, take **Rice University** (an outstanding private university in Houston, Texas), where undergraduates are randomly assigned to one of 11 residential colleges—each with its own dining hall, public rooms, dorm rooms, and competitive website. In fact, about 75 percent of undergraduates continue to live in their residential college throughout their time at Rice. Each residential college has a faculty master, who lives in an adjacent house and promotes a rich intellectual and cultural life and a plan for self-governance at the residential college. Or take **Vassar College** (a well-respected private college in Poughkeepsie, New York), where about 98 percent of students live on campus and about 70 percent of faculty members also live on or near the campus. One or two faculty families live in each of Vassar's self-governing residence halls, eight of which are coeducational.

Many colleges have a mix of housing facilities, including off-campus apartment buildings owned and operated by the college. And then there are some colleges that do not offer housing at all—and not just two-year community colleges, many (but not all) of which expect students to commute to campus. For example, the **University of Massachusetts campus in Boston**, which is the only public four-year college in Boston, does not have dormitories for its students. Its Office of Student Housing does, however, assist students with looking for apartment housing nearby, finding roommates, and dealing with landlords.

> ✓ Go to **Questions 29 and 30**. Check off the types of housing that the college offers. Then, jot down any interesting housing information, including any statistics about how many students live in campus housing and for how long.

Commuting to Campus

If it is likely that you would commute from home to a college on your LLCO, then consider what the commute would be like for you. Think about whether you would be using public transportation and, if so, how frequently those buses, trains, or subways run during the day and at night. Think about what traffic and parking would be like if you were driving your own car to the campus. Think about what the commute would be like in bad weather. Consider the cost of commuting as well—unless the college is within walking distance, of course.

> ✓ Go to **Question 31**. Jot down what your commute would be like if you plan to commute to the college from home.

STEP 11: RESEARCH THE COLLEGE'S SECURITY MEASURES

Step 11 brings us to the safety of students on campus and the security measures that a college takes to keep its students safe. You probably think a lot less about this topic than your parents do, but getting information about security measures on campus is one way to help alleviate your parents' concerns about your going away to college and living on campus. You can get necessary information on each college's website and from College Navigator to answer **Questions 32, 33, and 34** on **Security Measures**. You will also notice and definitely hear about security measures if you visit a college and take a campus tour.

Before we go on, let's say a word to those of you who plan to commute to campus from home. Safety is an issue for you, too. You will still need to pay attention to all of the security measures on campus, just as a residential student will do. But you will also have to worry about the convenience and safety of the commute.

What about late-night trips home after a meeting on campus or a late class or studying in the library? What about the safety of getting to a remote parking lot to get in your car or the safety of waiting for 20 minutes or more on a subway platform or on an empty street for a public bus? What about commuting in bad weather, especially in snowstorms, when a college campus might close down unexpectedly and public transportation is snarled? Safety issues might be even more important for commuters, and the college cannot be responsible for the safety of your commute once you leave the campus.

Security Measures

If you are going to live on campus and you have a chance to visit a campus housing facility, **notice whether there is an adult uniformed security guard with a sign-in and sign-out book at the entrance of that residential facility**. Ask whether the security guard is there 24 hours a day. We know that many college students find these security guards to be a bit annoying, and we know that this amount of supervision is one reason some students prefer to move into off-campus housing after the freshman year. But, we can also tell you that parents love seeing those security guards at the entrances to residential facilities, and we don't blame them.

Obviously, uniformed guards provide a higher level of security than a reception desk staffed by students who are working part-time jobs or work-study jobs. Some colleges, in fact, do not have anyone at all on duty to monitor the flow of people in and out of residential facilities; students just go in and out with their own keys or cards.

Whether you are on a campus tour or reading about a college on a website, look for daytime and nighttime security measures:

- **Many colleges use shuttle buses or vans** to take students from one part of campus to another, especially

when the campus is big. They are not only safer than having a student walk a long way alone, but also warmer or cooler and drier, if the weather is not cooperating.
- **Many colleges have blue-light call boxes on recognizable stand-alone towers with a blue light on top**, which are placed along walkways, in parking lots, or in distant parts of the campus. They let a student in trouble call for help instantly. Some are also outfitted with cameras, sirens, and broadcast systems to alert students nearby or to provide more information for the police or security guards. Some colleges believe that these blue-light call boxes deter criminal activity; all colleges believe they are a good thing to be able to advertise to prospective students and their parents.
- **Some colleges provide students to serve as walking escorts** from building to building or from buildings to the parking lots after dark, for obvious reasons.

And some colleges have all of the above and more. As any parent would say, "The more, the better."

Here are some more questions you should research:
- Are there security guards at the entrances to all of the classroom buildings, libraries, auditoriums, sports facilities, and so on?
- Are student IDs needed to get in and out of campus buildings?
- How do guests and visitors get in and out of campus buildings?
- Is the campus gated or fenced in or walled in or otherwise closed off? Are there guards at the campus entrances? As your research will show, many urban campuses do not have any enclosed campus to speak of; they are more like a collection of buildings in a group of city blocks, but without a definable campus. It's harder to provide a sense of security in those cases. But access to the campus is not just an urban issue. On suburban and rural campuses, is it possible for those outside of the college community to wander on and off the campus at will? That can be just as dangerous as any urban setting.

> ✓ Go to **Question 32.** Check off the types of security measures that the college provides on campus.

Crime Statistics

Now, go to College Navigator and look under *Campus Security* for each college on your LLCO. There you will find crime statistics for three years, including the number of criminal offenses and reasons for arrests on the campus and, specifically, in the residence halls. Though you and your parents probably do not have any experience interpreting crime statistics, you can compare the statistics from college to college to get an idea of whether some colleges on your LLCO seem safer than others.

> ✓ Go to **Question 33.** Jot down any crime statistics that seem noteworthy.

News Stories About Safety Issues

As you probably know, there have been stories in the news recently about safety issues on college campuses. Some of these stories have brought to light incidents of female students being sexually assaulted or harassed by other students. Sometimes it is not clear what degree of responsibility the colleges in these stories have taken or should have taken for the incidents that have been reported. While it is not fair to blame a college for the actions of an individual student, it is fair to look at whether a college has a culture or habit of being unresponsive to students' claims and complaints, particularly about sexual misconduct. These news stories, if reported in reliable media, are worth considering when choosing a college.

> ✓ Go to **Question 34.** Jot down details from any reliable news stories about student safety incidents at the college.

STEP 12: RESEARCH THE COLLEGE'S ACTIVITIES AND SPORTS

Step 12 asks you to investigate what the colleges on your LLCO have to offer outside of the classroom—extracurricular activities, community service activities, fraternities and sororities, and intercollegiate and intramural sports. These activities that will help enrich your life outside of the classroom can make the difference between a great college experience and a just-okay college experience for you. You will need to go to each college's website to research this topic and to answer **Questions 35-39** on **Activities and Sports**.

Extracurricular Activities

Many of you participated in extracurricular activities in high school. Some of you did that because you really enjoyed the activities, and some of you did that because you thought it would help you get into a good college. Whatever your reasons were in high school, **extracurricular activities in college will increase your network of friends, give you something worthwhile to do in your free time, give your mind a break from academics, and possibly lead to a career or to a hobby that could last a lifetime.** College is truly more than academics.

When we did our virtual college tour, it was astounding to us just how many activities are available on most college campuses, and it seemed clear that a student could start a club for almost any purpose that interested him or her if such a club did not already exist. It was not uncommon to find that large universities had literally hundreds and hundreds of student activities and clubs—truly, something for everyone. There is everything you had in high school, plus so much more—theater groups, music groups, newspapers, yearbooks, literary magazines, student government organizations, agricultural organizations, engineering associations, honor societies, and so on.

On most college websites, you will find a long, long, long list of these activities and clubs, usually with descriptions about what they do. So, think hard about what you like to do now. Then, think about what might be interesting, but you haven't had the chance to try it yet. See what the colleges on your LLCO offer and imagine yourself becoming involved.

Don't underestimate the importance of activities—either now in high school or later in college. Keep in mind that some college applications ask you to write an essay about your most important high school activity and that many college applications ask you whether you plan to continue with your various activities once you get to college. It's a good idea to say "yes."

> ✓ Go to **Question 35**. Jot down how many extracurricular activities the college offers and list some that you are interested in.

Community Service Activities

Many of you participated in community service activities in high school. Some of you did that because you really enjoyed the activities, some of you did that because your high school required it, and some of you did that because you thought it would help you get into a good college. Whatever your reasons were in high school, **community service activities in college will increase your network of friends, give you something worthwhile to do in your free time, give your mind a break from academics, and possibly lead to a career or to a way of life that could last a lifetime.** Again, college is truly more than academics, and what is more important than doing something to help someone else.

When we did our virtual college tour, we found quite a few colleges that place a strong emphasis on community service, including some colleges that require it. Some faith-based institutions, like Jesuit institutions, are especially concerned with outreach to the community. For example, Global Outreach (GO!) at **Fordham University** in New York City is a program that sends teams of students and chaperones during school breaks to live simply, work, and learn about poverty and social injustice in communities in 30 locations in and outside the U.S.

Since 2006, the President's Higher Education Community Service Honor Roll recognizes colleges that have outstanding community service programs. You can see whether the colleges on your LLCO have ever won the Honor Roll's Presidential Award for dedication to community outreach, to service learning, and to civic engagement.

On most college websites, you will find a section about community outreach or community service. See what the colleges on your LLCO believe and have to offer. Then, think hard about the value of these activities to others and what you can learn yourself.

> ✓ Go to **Question 36**. Jot down how many community service activities the college offers and list some that you are interested in.

Fraternities and Sororities

For some students, fraternities and sororities are a big part of their college lives. **They act as a social hub, but also typically offer personal support, academic support, community service opportunities, and often great housing options.** Many colleges offer a large number of fraternities and sororities (often referred to as "Greek life"), and many offer a smaller number of them. There are also black sororities and fraternities, which have their own substantial history, traditions, and purposes. Depending on the college, fraternities and sororities play a larger or smaller role in the college environment. Some colleges, by the way, do not offer any fraternities and sororities at all.

Wanting to join a fraternity or sorority might be one thing that has been passed down to you from your parents. If your parents went to college and were fraternity/sorority members, chances are that you are interested in joining, too. If your parents did not go to college or were not fraternity/sorority members, this is a part of college life that you should investigate before deciding one way or the other.

While we can't imagine that the presence of fraternities and sororities would be the reason to choose a college to attend, it could be one thing you put on the scale when weighing your choices.

> ✓ Go to **Question 37**. Check off whether the college has fraternities and sororities.

Intercollegiate and Intramural Sports

For some students, intercollegiate athletics is the reason to go to college, and an athletic scholarship is paying the full cost of the college experience. If you are in line for such a scholarship, good for you. However, that is certainly not the case for most students. So, what about the rest of you?

Well, you can still play on an intercollegiate sports team. Many colleges have 25 or more such teams—some men's, some women's, and some coeducational. If you try to research the available teams, you are likely to find yourself redirected to a different website—that is, one specifically for intercollegiate athletics. You will easily find all of the teams, news about them, ticket information, merchandise to purchase, and more. **Remember that playing on an intercollegiate sports team is a serious commitment—physically, mentally, and emotionally—and you have to be both talented and hardworking to make most intercollegiate teams.**

Of course, intercollegiate sports is not just for the players, but also for the fans. Some students want to go to a college that offers the fun of football weekends, basketball fever, ice hockey fanaticism, lacrosse dynasties, and more. Attending soccer and baseball games or swimming and track meets or gymnastics competitions can become an extracurricular activity in itself. And there is nothing wrong with that!

If you enjoy sports as a hobby (including as a passionate hobby), then look for the intramural teams and club sports that most colleges offer. The variety of sports available can be amazing, and the number of such teams can surpass the number of intercollegiate teams. Many colleges strongly encourage students to participate in these sports activities for a variety of physical, mental, and emotional health reasons. Intramural teams and clubs are one more way to make new friends on a campus—and stay healthy.

> ✓ Go to **Questions 38 and 39.** Jot down the number of intercollegiate sports that the college has, along with any that you are interested in. Then, do the same for intramural and club sports.

STEP 13:
RESEARCH THE COLLEGE'S ADMISSION PRACTICES

Well, this is where it gets serious. Researching Step 13 will give you an idea about how likely you are to be accepted by a college if you decide to apply. Of course, no one can say for sure whether your grades or admission test scores or extracurricular and community service activities or letters of recommendation will be appealing enough to get you admitted to a particular college. But several academic hurdles might turn out to be what stands between you and one or more colleges on your LLCO. You will need to use both each college's website and College Navigator to research this crucial topic and to answer **Questions 40-49** on **Admission Practices**.

To get started, **you need to figure out whether the data you are examining are for "admitted" students or for "enrolled freshmen."** These two groups are obviously not the same because many students who are admitted to a college do not actually enroll. Since you are trying to figure out whether you will be admitted, using "admitted" student data, when available, is probably the better choice; however, either set of data will give you an idea of the caliber of the applicants a college accepts.

Start by looking up the colleges on your LLCO on College Navigator and going to the *Admissions* section of the college profile. These data will be for "enrolled first-time students." Helpful data are presented clearly in this section.

Then check each college's website. Some colleges do a great job of presenting data on admitted students or enrolled freshmen, and others simply do not. Some colleges make it easy by providing a page of facts and figures about the new freshman class—sometimes called a *Class Profile* (of students who enrolled) or an *Admitted Student Profile* (of students who were admitted, but did not necessarily enroll). However, it is not always easy to locate this page (though it is often in the *Admission* section of the website). If you can find the common data set on the website, you will want to look under the third part: *C. First-Time, First-Year (Freshman) Admission*.

> ✓ Go to **Question 40**. Check off whether the data you will be using are for admitted students or for enrolled freshmen. In a few cases, you might find data on both.

Acceptance Rate

One way to judge the selectivity of a college is by looking at the number of students it accepts compared to the number of students who applied. Let's call this "acceptance rate." You should understand that, generally speaking, **colleges like to boast that they have a low acceptance rate; that makes them feel more exclusive.** There are many ways for a college to manipulate its acceptance rate, such as by encouraging applicants who are really not qualified and who will be rejected when they apply—a practice that is just as mean-spirited as it sounds. There have even been some news stories, opinion columns, and general criticism lately of colleges that seem overly impressed with their own super-low acceptance rates—say, below 10 percent.

Without looking too closely at small differences in acceptance rates (like the difference in selectivity of a college with a 15 percent acceptance rate and a college with an 18 percent acceptance rate), you should know that **the higher that acceptance rate is, the better chance you probably have of being admitted**. While some well-known top-ranked private colleges have acceptance rates below 20 percent, some well-respected high-ranked private colleges and great public flagship universities have acceptance rates closer to 30 percent. And other excellent public flagship universities have acceptance rates closer to 50 percent. In fact, you will find some colleges with acceptance rates higher than that.

So, check out the *Percent admitted* line on the College Navigator profile. Or calculate the percent admitted for yourself, using the available data for men and women separately from the first four lines (*C1*) in the common data set. Keep in mind that you will want to have some colleges on your LLCO with acceptance rates around 40 percent or better—just to be safe.

> ✓ Go to **Question 41**. Jot down the percent of applicants admitted to the college.

High School Grade Point Average (GPA)

For many, but not all, colleges, you will be able to find the full distribution of high school GPAs and the average high school GPA of the students enrolled in the freshman class by looking under *C11* and *C12* of the common data set on the college's website. You also might find it on a *Class Profile* sheet on the website, but you will not find this information on College Navigator.

This average high school GPA will be on a 4-point scale. For example, a great college might show an average high school GPA of 3.8, meaning that its enrolled freshmen did extremely well in their high school courses.

As Advanced Placement and International Baccalaureate courses have become increasingly popular and as more high schools have started to "weight" students' grades in those courses (and sometimes in their own honors courses as well), there has been a rise in high school GPAs. In other words, when a student in a high school with weighted grades gets an A in a regular course, that A is worth a 4.0, or 4 points. But if a student in a high school with weighted grades gets an A in an Advanced Placement course, that A is worth a 5.0, or 5 points—that is, the grade has more "weight."

Whether your high school does or does not weight course grades is something that should be part of the high school narrative profile that your school's counselor will send off to colleges with your high school transcript. That profile is helpful to colleges in judging your GPA.

Nonetheless, **one effect of all of this weighting of high school course grades appears to be that average high school GPAs of incoming freshmen are on the rise**. We can tell this anecdotally by the fact that many colleges we profiled in our virtual college tour, including some not super-selective ones, post surprisingly high average GPAs well over a 3.5 for the incoming freshman class.

So, look carefully at the average high school GPAs that colleges are putting out there and see how yours compares. And, remember, some colleges will not provide one.

> ✓ Go to **Question 42**. Jot down the average high school GPA of enrolled freshmen.

High School Class Rank

For many, but not all, colleges, you will be able to find the full distribution of high school class ranks of the students enrolled in the freshman class by looking under *C10* of the common data set on a college's website; there you will also find the percent of students who actually submitted a class rank. *C10* will tell you the percent of students who were in the top tenth, top quarter, top half, bottom half, and bottom quarter of their high school graduating class (these categories are obviously overlapping).

You also might find class rank information on a *Class Profile* sheet on the website, where one college we profiled actually publicized the number of enrolled students who were named valedictorian (a #1 class rank) of their graduating class—and it was a big number! You will not, however, find class rank information on College Navigator.

There have been a number of stories in the education media lately about school districts that do not want to name valedictorians any longer. Why? Because they have found that the competition for that spot sometimes comes down to a thousandth of a point in that GPA we just discussed. Furthermore, they have found that students are so focused on getting that extra-high GPA that they will actually NOT take high school courses they would otherwise have taken in order to broaden their studies—or should take in order to prepare for college—for fear of hurting their GPAs. That is a crying shame.

Of course, for many years, some high schools have simply not provided class ranks for a variety of reasons, and it is not a requirement from any government office or governing body that high schools must provide class ranks. Similarly, some colleges will simply say that class ranks are not available for admitted or enrolled freshmen.

> ✓ Go to **Question 43**. Jot down whatever information you find on the distribution of students by class rank.

Test-Optional or Test-Flexible Colleges

The college website is usually quite clear about whether a college is a test-optional college (meaning that students do not have to submit college admission test scores) or a test-flexible college (meaning that students are given a choice of various types of test scores to submit).

However, we have noticed that many colleges that do not require the submission of SAT or ACT scores receive them, nonetheless, from many applicants. Because those scores are usually quite good, it is evident that students with good scores do, in fact, supply them to test-optional colleges. How those scores figure into admissions decisions is anybody's guess. Here is our advice: **If you have good SAT or ACT scores, you should probably submit them to test-optional colleges, even though they are not required.**

There are perhaps only a handful of colleges that say that they absolutely do NOT want any test scores sent to them and that they will NOT use them at all for any reason, including well-regarded **Hampshire College**, which makes a crystal clear statement on its website about this subject.

> ✓ Go to **Question 44**. Check off whether the college is a test-optional or test-flexible college.

SAT and ACT Scores

In part *C9*, the common data set does a good job of providing the following testing data:

- **The percent of students who submitted SAT and ACT scores**
- **The SAT and ACT scores, by subtest, at the 25th percentile of students and at the 75th percentile of students** (in other words, 25 percent of students scored at or below the score at the 25th percentile, and 25 percent of students scored at or above the score at the 75th percentile)
- **The full distribution of SAT and ACT scores, by subtest**

College Navigator also provides most of this information, if that is easier for you to get to than the common data set. Some college websites also provide the actual average, or "mean," admission test score, and that can be handy, too.

If your scores fall above the 75th percentile of scores for a college's students, that is good. If your scores fall right in the middle between the 25th percentile and the 75th percentile, that would be just about average for a college's students. But if your scores fall close to or below the 25th percentile, that would not be nearly so promising in terms of your chances of being admitted.

Remember, even if the college you are researching has declared itself to be a test-optional college, it might provide SAT and ACT information for those students who chose to submit test scores, and that information will be helpful to you.

> ✓ Go to **Questions 45 and 46**. Jot down the SAT and ACT scores, by subtest.

SAT Subject Tests

In part *C8A*, the common data set records whether SAT Subject Tests are either required or recommended for admission. It does not, however, tell you how many Subject Tests are required or what specific Subject Tests (if any) are required. For that information, you will need to go to the college's website. College Navigator does not have any specific information on this topic.

> ✓ Go to **Question 47**. Check off whether any SAT Subject Tests are either required or recommended for admission and, if required, the specifics about those tests.

High School Courses

Let's look at one last admission standard—one that is less often considered and more often taken for granted—and that is the courses that applicants are expected to have taken in high school, usually listed in terms of credits (or Carnegie units) in each subject area, but also sometimes including specific courses, especially in math and science.

Part *C5* of the common data set displays both REQUIRED and RECOMMENDED high school units, by subject area, but you should check out each college's website for more detailed information. College Navigator does not have any specific information on this topic.

On a college's website, this information can virtually always be found by starting with the *Admission* home page. You will find that **the high school course or credit expectations of colleges do, in fact, differ, usually according to how selective the college is**. But there are always a few surprises (like colleges that require students to have earned career and technical education credits in high school, for example).

After you write down the required and the recommended courses or credits, you can compare them from college to college, and you can see how well they match up with what you have taken so far and with what you will be taking as you finish up high school. Particularly if you are just a freshman or sophomore, this information can be invaluable as you plan your remaining semesters in high school. For example, what if a college on your LLCO requires—or, more likely, recommends—four credits of foreign language? Foreign language is something that lots of high school students drop out of before taking a fourth year. Perhaps that's because they don't know how many selective colleges recommend it.

The courses that you take in high school matter, including the courses that you take in your senior year. Colleges will tell you that slacking off in the senior year is never a good move. So, for example, a fourth year of math and a fourth year of science would be the best scenario for most applicants—and might be a mandatory scenario for entrance to top colleges and to some college programs, like engineering. If you don't have a rigorous senior year planned, think again.

> ✓ Go to **Questions 48 and 49**. Jot down the number of high school credits/courses that are required and, separately, that are recommended in each subject. In addition, jot down any specific courses that are required or recommended.

STEP 14:
RESEARCH THE COLLEGE'S COST

Step 14 is the last step and, to many people, the most important step. We hope that it is NOT the most important step to you when deciding where to apply, however, simply because it is very hard to predict what financial aid you might be able to get from a college, from your state government, from the federal government, and from outside organizations. It is also true that financial aid at a good private college on your LLCO could make that college as affordable as any good public university on your LLCO. But that is something you won't know before you apply. We understand that paying attention to cost is a sensible thing to do—it's just not the only thing.

Tuition and Fees

College Navigator offers a straightforward table of college costs under the heading *Tuition, Fees, and Estimated Student Expenses*. You can certainly use it, at least to compare the colleges on your LLCO.

However, you should probably go directly to each college's website to research costs instead because College Navigator will have the college costs for the preceding year and will not have the college costs for either the current year or, more important to you, the upcoming year. **Be advised that college website material on tuition and fees can be harder to find than you might expect and can be difficult to understand.**

Depending on what time of year you do your research, you might be looking at the current year's figures or next year's figures. Use the most up-to-date information you can find. However, to be fair when comparing the colleges on your LLCO, it will help if all of the figures are for the same academic year.

Some websites display tuition and fees separately; some provide one combined figure. **Try to use a combined tuition-plus-fees figure for each college so that the figures will be comparable from college to college.**

One last word of caution: **Some websites display information by term (e.g., by semester, by quarter), while others display information for the full academic year.** Make sure you know which you are reading! For example, remember to multiply by 2, if the information you see is for just one semester.

> ✓ **Go to Question 50.** Jot down the tuition and fees for the current academic year or, if possible, for the next academic year. Record the year, too.

Tuition Incentives

Some colleges have attractive and even compelling tuition incentives, which they will proudly announce on their websites—usually in the same place as the tuition information. For example, **some colleges freeze tuition** for four years at the price you start with as a freshman. **Some colleges allow students to take an extra semester for free** if the college is at fault for not offering, on an accessible enough schedule, all of the courses needed to graduate on time in four years. **Some colleges provide generous discounts to students from contiguous states or to students in the region** (like the West or the Midwest or New England). It makes sense to see whether each college on your LLCO has any tuition discount that could help you at any point in your undergraduate years.

> ✓ Go to **Question 51**. Jot down any tuition incentives.

Residential Housing Costs

College Navigator provides figures for on-campus room and board in the same spot as tuition and fees. Again, however, this information is for the preceding academic year. So, again, it is best to get residential housing costs from each college's website for the current year or for the next year.

Obviously, this housing cost is important if you are planning to live on campus and especially important if a college requires freshmen to live on campus. Even if you think you might commute to a college on your LLCO, it won't hurt to jot down this information, just in case you change your mind.

You might find a range of housing costs, depending on which facility you want to live in, on whether you want a single room, on what kind of meal plan you prefer, and more. Try to write down the cost for the same type of living situation at each college so that you can compare college costs later.

> ✓ Go to **Question 52**. Jot down the residential housing costs for room and board for freshman year.

NOW, IT'S UP TO YOU

You have done a lot of work to gather information about the colleges on your LLCO. You have completed a **College Profile Worksheet** on quite a few colleges by now. You have learned more than many high school students know about a variety of specific colleges and about higher education generally.

So, it's time to start comparing and contrasting the colleges you have researched. That will be a long process, which will require analysis and evaluation by you and your parents and perhaps other important family members. And it's okay that it is a long process because this is a big decision for all of you.

Remember that choosing which colleges to apply to can be every bit as important as choosing which college to attend. In an ideal world, you should be happy with every college you apply to because that will take the pressure off as you wait for acceptances to come in.

Of course, you might be more excited about some choices than others, but don't apply to any college that you would not want to attend. That is a waste of your time and money. **We are confident that there is a college that you can be admitted to that will make you happy.** Even safety schools don't have to be disappointing choices. If they are for you now, you just haven't looked hard enough yet! Get busy.

ABOUT THE AUTHORS

About Regina H. Paul

During my career at Policy Studies in Education, my nonprofit organization, I have worked hard to improve K–12 public education. I have developed K–12 curricula in all subjects, developed student examinations for school districts and states, evaluated new programs in over 400 school districts, and done market studies for over 150 colleges. I have consulted for state legislatures, state boards of education, state education departments, and foundations.

Recently, I served as the chief consultant in the design and establishment of New York City's first public Early College high school with a career and technical education focus. Our school created an innovative trimester system that enabled students to complete high school in three years instead of four. As we got ready to send our students off to college (many a year early), we discovered they needed guidance. We gave it to them, one by one. Now, this book will do the same thing, but will allow us to reach many more students. Nothing is more important than giving all high school students the guidance they need to make a great college choice.

About Marie G. Segares

I bring over 10 years of experience as an education manager and college professor to my role as co-host of the *USACollegeChat* podcast. I've worked in academic affairs in both a public and a private college and in student affairs in a large university. I have taught at several institutions of higher education—in the U.S. and abroad—both in online and face-to-face classes, both in undergraduate and graduate courses.

I've always been passionate about increasing access to college for a diverse group of students. Working with parents and students as a co-founder of a public Early College high school in New York City and as the director of its Early College program introduced me to many hard-working families who needed more information about the world of college and were overwhelmed by the many options. I have enjoyed sharing my experiences—as an alumna of three institutions of higher education, as an education manager, and as a college instructor—on the *USACollegeChat* podcast every week.

About Policy Studies in Education

For over 40 years, Policy Studies in Education has provided consulting services and technical assistance to schools, local and state boards of education, state education departments, state legislatures, federal education agencies, foundations, professional education associations, and public and private colleges. We have conducted more than 500 data-based studies and program design projects in more than 40 states and abroad. These projects have spanned an array of topics, including curriculum and test development, program development and evaluation, parent advocacy, school governance, policy formulation and analysis, and administrative organization. In addition, we have trained tens of thousands of teachers and administrators and school board members across the U.S. We are proud to sponsor *USACollegeChat*, a free weekly podcast designed to help parents and students understand the world of college options (episodes are available at http://usacollegechat.org and on Google Play Music, iTunes, Stitcher, and TuneIn).

HOW TO EXPLORE YOUR COLLEGE OPTIONS

YOUR LONG LIST OF COLLEGE OPTIONS

Cut along the dotted line to make it easier to use and copy this worksheet. Permission is granted by the publisher to reproduce this worksheet for individual use only. Permission is not granted for resale or distribution. For institutional use, contact info@policystudies.org. © 2017 Policy Studies in Education.

1. _____
2. _____
3. _____
4. _____
5. _____
6. _____
7. _____
8. _____
9. _____
10. _____
11. _____
12. _____
13. _____
14. _____
15. _____
16. _____
17. _____
18. _____
19. _____
20. _____
21. _____
22. _____
23. _____
24. _____
25. _____
26. _____
27. _____
28. _____
29. _____
30. _____

HOW TO EXPLORE YOUR COLLEGE OPTIONS

COLLEGE PROFILE WORKSHEET

Cut along the dotted line to make it easier to use and copy this worksheet. Permission is granted by the publisher to reproduce this worksheet for individual use only. Permission is not granted for resale or distribution. For institutional use, contact info@policystudies.org. © 2017 Policy Studies in Education.

College name: _____

HISTORY AND MISSION

1. **Brief history of the college:**

   _____
   _____
   _____
   _____
   _____
   _____
   _____
   _____
   _____
   _____
   _____
   _____
   _____

2. **Claims about the college (e.g., "firsts," top-ranked departments):**

   _____
   _____
   _____
   _____
   _____
   _____

3. **Public/private status of the college today:**

   ☐ Public
   ☐ Private nonprofit/not-for-profit
   ☐ Public-private partnership
   ☐ Private for-profit

4. Any special mission of the college today:
   - ☐ Faith-based college or university
   - ☐ HBCU (Historically Black College or University)
   - ☐ HSI (Hispanic-Serving Institution)
   - ☐ Single-sex college or university

LOCATION

5. College location (city and state): _____

6. Type of community the college is located in:
   - ☐ Urban
   - ☐ Suburban
   - ☐ Rural
   - ☐ Small town

7. Information and advertising claims about the community and surrounding area, including natural beauty, historic sites, entertainment venues, restaurants, recreation opportunities, etc.:

_____
_____
_____
_____
_____
_____
_____
_____
_____
_____
_____
_____
_____
_____
_____

© 2017 *Policy Studies in Education.*

ENROLLMENT

8. Undergraduate enrollment: _____

9. Breakdown of undergraduate students by full-time *vs.* part-time attendance:

    _____% Attending full time

    _____% Attending part time

10. Breakdown of undergraduate students by gender:

    _____% Female

    _____% Male

    Other gender identity information or policies:

    _____
    _____
    _____
    _____
    _____

11. Breakdown of undergraduate students by race/ethnicity:

    _____% American Indian or Alaska Native

    _____% Asian

    _____% Black or African American

    _____% Hispanic or Latino

    _____% Native Hawaiian or Other Pacific Islander

    _____% White

    _____% Two or more races

    _____% Race/ethnicity unknown/not reported

12. **Breakdown of undergraduate students by student residence:**

    _____% From the state where the college is located (in-state)

    _____% From other states (out-of-state)

    _____% From foreign countries

    Other interesting facts about where students come from:

    _____
    _____
    _____
    _____

© 2017 Policy Studies in Education.

13. Support services for specific groups of undergraduate students, including students of color, first-generation-to-college students, LGBTQ students, students with learning disabilities, etc.:

    _____
    _____
    _____
    _____
    _____
    _____
    _____
    _____
    _____
    _____
    _____

14. Retention rate from freshman to sophomore year: _____%

15. Graduation rates for students pursuing bachelor's degrees:

    _____% In 4 years

    _____% In 6 years

16. Graduate enrollment (if any): _____

CLASS SIZE

17. Student-to-faculty ratio: _____ -to-1

18. Information and advertising claims about class size:

    _____
    _____
    _____
    _____
    _____
    _____
    _____
    _____

© 2017 *Policy Studies in Education.*

ACADEMICS

19. Schools and/or colleges within the institution, if it is a university or institute (check off the ones that serve undergraduate students and double check the ONE that you are most interested in applying to):

_____
_____
_____
_____
_____
_____
_____
_____
_____
_____
_____
_____

20. Names of several academic departments that you are interested in:

_____
_____
_____
_____
_____
_____

21. Names of several majors that you are interested in:

_____
_____
_____
_____
_____

© 2017 *Policy Studies in Education.*

22. Does the college have a core curriculum or general education curriculum or distribution requirements?

☐ No
☐ Yes

If yes, jot down the exact requirements listed on the website—whether they are specific courses, or a number of courses in specific academic subjects (e.g., philosophy), or a number of courses in groups of academic subjects (e.g., arts, humanities), or all three:

_____
_____
_____
_____
_____
_____
_____

23. Study abroad options (locations, programs, and important details):

_____
_____
_____
_____
_____
_____

24. Does the college have a traditional numerical or letter grading system for assignments, exams, and final course grades?

☐ Yes
☐ No

If no, jot down the way that students are graded (e.g., with written narrative evaluations where professors comment on strengths and weaknesses):

_____
_____
_____
_____

© 2017 Policy Studies in Education.

SCHEDULE

25. Number of weeks courses last: _____

26. Type of term:

- ☐ Semesters
- ☐ Trimesters
- ☐ Quarters
- ☐ Something else: _____

27. A description of any innovative scheduling at the college:

_____
_____
_____
_____
_____
_____
_____
_____
_____
_____
_____
_____

HOUSING

28. Are freshmen required to live in on-campus residential housing?

☐ Yes   ☐ No

29. Types of housing that the college offers:

- ☐ Traditional dormitories
- ☐ Apartment-style suites
- ☐ Residential "houses"
- ☐ Off-campus apartments owned and operated by the college
- ☐ Something else: _____
- ☐ No housing available

© 2017 Policy Studies in Education.

30. **Any interesting information about housing, housing requirements, how many years students typically stay in campus housing, or what percentage of students live in campus housing:**

_____
_____
_____
_____
_____

31. **A description of what your commute would be like if you were commuting to the college from home:**

_____
_____
_____

SECURITY MEASURES

32. **Types of security that the college provides on campus:**
    - ☐ Uniformed security guards at housing facilities
    - ☐ Non-uniformed desk attendants at housing facilities
    - ☐ Blue-light call boxes
    - ☐ Uniformed security guards at classroom buildings, libraries, auditoriums, sports facilities, etc.
    - ☐ Walking escorts
    - ☐ Shuttle buses/vans on campus
    - ☐ Gated/fenced/walled campus
    - ☐ Something else: _____

33. **Any noteworthy crime statistics from College Navigator:**

_____
_____
_____
_____

34. **Any details from reliable news stories about safety issues on campus (e.g., sexual assaults):**

_____
_____
_____

© 2017 Policy Studies in Education.

ACTIVITIES AND SPORTS

35. Number of extracurricular activities and any ones you are interested in:

_____
_____
_____
_____
_____

36. Number of community service activities and any ones you are interested in:

_____
_____
_____
_____
_____

37. Are there fraternities and sororities?

☐ Yes ☐ No

38. Number of intercollegiate sports and any ones you are interested in:

_____
_____
_____

39. Number of intramural or club sports and any ones you are interested in:

_____
_____
_____

ADMISSION PRACTICES

40. Are data provided for admitted students or for enrolled freshmen?

☐ Admitted students ☐ Enrolled freshmen

41. Percent of applicants who were admitted: _____%

42. Average high school GPA: _____

© 2017 *Policy Studies in Education.*

43. **Distribution of students by class rank (e.g., percentage of students in the top tenth of their senior class, and so on):**

_____
_____
_____
_____
_____
_____

44. **Is the college a test-optional or test-flexible college?**
    ☐ Yes, test-optional   ☐ Yes, test-flexible   ☐ No, tests required

45. **SAT scores in reading and math (and writing, if available) at the 25th and 75th percentiles and average SAT scores (if available):**

_____
_____
_____
_____
_____
_____

46. **ACT scores in English, math, and writing as well as the composite scores at the 25th and 75th percentiles and average ACT scores (if available):**

_____
_____
_____
_____
_____

47. **Are SAT Subject Tests required?**
    ☐ Yes, required   ☐ No, but recommended   ☐ No, neither one

    If required or recommended, how many Subject Tests and which ones?

_____
_____
_____

© 2017 *Policy Studies in Education.*

48. **Number of credits/courses REQUIRED for admission to the college or to the college/school that you are interested in within the university AND any specific courses required (e.g., Biology, Algebra II):**

ENGLISH _____

MATH _____

SCIENCE _____

SOCIAL STUDIES _____

FOREIGN LANGUAGES _____

ARTS _____

OTHER _____

49. **Number of credits/courses RECOMMENDED, in addition to those required, for admission to the college or to the college/school that you are interested in within the university AND any specific courses recommended (e.g., Calculus):**

ENGLISH _____

MATH _____

SCIENCE _____

SOCIAL STUDIES _____

FOREIGN LANGUAGES _____

ARTS _____

OTHER _____

COST

50. Tuition and fees for the _____ academic year *(fill in the year)*:

_____

_____

51. Any tuition incentives (e.g., tuition frozen for four years, discounts for nearby students):

_____

_____

_____

52. Residential housing costs for room and board for freshman year:

_____

_____

© 2017 *Policy Studies in Education.*

Made in the USA
Middletown, DE
22 April 2019